MW01290468

B♥Y Bye

Beautiful women
Finding their way back

**A woman's love is a man's privilege,
not his right.**

♥ *Unknown*

Copyright © 2013 Rhonda Hall
All rights reserved.
ISBN: 1478295848
ISBN 13: 9781478295846
Library of Congress Control Number: 2012913472
CreateSpace Independent Publishing Platform
North Charleston, South Carolina

This book is dedicated to all of the beautiful women who have the boldness to not settle, the courage to walk and stay away from relationships that are simply not good enough for them, and the confidence to stay fierce, strong, fly, and sassy through it all.

#IAmRockinASpiritOfGratitude

I am grateful for all of the relationships I both needed and found the strength to say *Boy Bye!* to. I am grateful for each experience, each teacher, and every lesson.

I am grateful for all of my wonderful and amazing friends who continuously provide much-needed encouragement in all forms and fashions—laughter, listening ears, motivating words, girls' nights out, and more.

I am grateful for my parents, my brother, my sister-cousins, my sister-friends, and my entire family for always being in my corner. Their continued love and support provide me with an unwavering sense of security in an insecure world.

I am grateful for being the child of a Heavenly Father who extends blessings, love, grace, and mercy on me even though I am not worthy of His faithfulness, kindness, and goodness.

Boy Bye! Contents

Frustrated Inspiration: Enough is Enough!

A grown woman knows when to let you go.

♥ *Raheem Devaughn*

*I*t wasn't a simple case of just another relationship biting the dust. This was the relationship that had held so much promise, so much potential. He was supposed to be *the one*. I thought my search for Mr. Right and happily-ever-after was finally over. I was hopeful that I'd kissed my final frog and at last, found my Prince. We talked about wedding styles and preferences occasionally. I was a fan of destination weddings held on beautiful beaches or at luxurious resorts. He, being more traditional and conservative, preferred a church wedding. He questioned the financial feasibility of a destination wedding for family members who had little ones in tow. And we couldn't forget about his aunt who was terrified of flying.

But somewhere in between the hypothetical planning and a concrete proposal, reality must have kicked in for him, because he couldn't bring himself to do it; he couldn't bring himself to ask for my hand in marriage; he couldn't bring himself to marry me (to my total disbelief) even after four years of courtship. Maybe the reality of being a married man, of being totally committed to someone else for the long haul and abandoning a carefree style of living, of accepting and fulfilling the roles required of a wedded man and the fear of marrying the wrong girl fueled by *perceived* pressure, was all just too overwhelming for him.

I wasn't trying to pressure him, though. I myself was at a personal crossroads. I could've unhappily stayed, continuing to give so much of myself and of my time and of my energy while not receiving what I really wanted in return—a full-fledged commitment as opposed to a playing-house commitment. In other words, I could have stayed and *settled*. Or…I could have checked myself out of the game playing wifey, found a spot on the sideline, and let a voluntary substitute player take my position over. I chose the latter; *we* chose the latter.

And although, in retrospect, I can truly appreciate his honesty, in the moment I was deeply hurt. I was thoroughly crushed and totally confused. Was my imagination sending me mixed signals the entire time? Did he not reapply for an employment position and relocate so we could be closer to each other? Was I somehow misled along the way? Were there red flags that I neglected or denied noticing? How did everything just swerve *way* left? This was *not* how our story was supposed to conclude—not my version anyway.

Nonetheless, after the ties were severed and the dust somewhat cleared, I was inspired to do something more than continue hosting countless, tear-filled, it-sucks-to-be-me, life-can't-go-on-without-him, did-I-make-the-right-decision, it-wasn't-*that*-bad-being-a-'good-enough'-girl (yes, it was) fests. I woke up one day feeling blue, feeling pissed off for *still* being pissed off even after several months of separation, and feeling inspired to write…something. But write what? I figured writing about my feelings at that current juncture in my life was a pretty good start. And once I started, it was hard to stop.

My personal experiences with love and disappointment were not the only inspiration for this book. It seemed as if *all* the women I knew directly (friends, family members, coworkers, neighbors), indirectly (friends of family members, friends of friends, family of friends) and even women I didn't know at all (entertainers, reality TV divas) were catching some form of relationship hell. In some instances, we were voluntarily wearing the catcher's mitt, catching all of relationship-hell's fastballs. We were relationship-hell enablers. And in other instances, we were thrown some unexpected, painful, shattering curveballs we could not have possibly seen coming. We took some hard and crushing emotional hits that we were simply not prepared for. Whether willing or unwilling participants in unhappy love, we were all passionately singing some line of "I'm In Relationship Hell."

I'm In Relationship Hell Lyrics

I think my man is cheating.

I don't think he's ever going to marry me.

I'm tired of being his side chick!

I don't know how much more of this I can take.

He's only interested in me for my body and my sex.

Why am I still with him?

I don't think he loves me anymore; he sure doesn't act like it.

He acts like he's doing *me* a favor by being with me.

He is not trying to settle down (not with me anyway).

I feel like I'm being strung along.

I *am* being strung along!

My relationship is making me miserable.

He's such a butthole!

This relationship sucks!

I'm selling myself short—way short.

I say I don't care if he cheats, but that's a lie; it really crushes my spirit.

I don't feel that I'm an important part of his life.

If you want out, just be a man about it and say so.

My relationship is draining me.

He doesn't seem to care about my feelings.

I cry every night.

I'm tired of his lies!

I don't believe anything that comes out of his mouth!

I feel like I'm the only one trying to make this work.

I'm not happy!

I'm settling.

I'm not happy!

I deserve better.

It started to become disheartening—very dis-heartening. All of us—beautiful women—selling ourselves way too short just to save face. All of us—beautiful women—being way too accommo-dating and way too compromising just so we can say, "I gotta man." All of us—beautiful women—granting a man and a relationship permission to assess our worth, determine our value, and vali-date who we are. All of us—beautiful women—lost in the haze of love. Jay-Z once said that he had to let the song cry, because he couldn't see them coming down his eyes. I let the pages cry, because I was sick and tired of tears coming down my eyes. They, my eyeballs, needed a break from releasing the salty-tasting liquid called tears. Actually, they deserved a super-duper, extended vacation…with pay!

A Formal Introduction to

Boy Bye!

Beautiful Women... Finding Their Way Back

You're beautiful like a flower, more

valuable than a diamond.

♥ India Arie

*B*oy Bye! is sincerely for all of us–beautiful women–finding our way back! Finding our way back *from* what? Finding our way back *to* what?

Finding our way back from the hurt, pain, and disappointment provoked by love; finding our way back from being emotionally knocked down for the count by a blow ironically called love; finding our way back from insecurities that have refused our eyes the privilege of seeing how beautiful we truly are; finding our way back from low self-esteem that has prevented us from fully understanding how special we genuinely are; finding our way back from attitudes that gave the men in our lives a free pass to treat us in a manner that is unacceptable and belittling, simply for fear of being alone; finding our way back from desperately seeking and being a slave to the approval and validation of others; finding our way back from feeling, believing, and behaving as if we're powerless; finding our way back from Timid Lane, Weak Street, Insecure

Avenue, Toleration Court, Fear Drive, Desperation Road, and Low-Self-Esteem-Having Boulevard; finding our way back to Strength Drive, Grace Court, Self-Love Lane, Confidence Way, Power Boulevard, Dignity Road, and Fearless Avenue; finding our way back to self-respect and dismissing all forms of disrespect; finding our way back to accepting, appreciating, and adoring ourselves despite our love-life status; finding our way back to embracing the "hot girls" we were born to be.

Boy Bye! encourages all women to repossess the joy they've been temporarily robbed of, to tune into how amazing and how special they absolutely are, to recognize just how much power they really possess, to elevate their standards and expectations for how they're to be treated in relationships, to boldly demand and anticipate *more* than mediocrity from the men they're involved with, to be confident enough to walk away from a relationship, and to be strong enough to be alone if the only other alternative is...to settle.

Boy Bye! is for all the beautiful women...finding their way back.

1

Done...D-O-N-E...Done!

I got a simple rule about everybody.

If you don't treat me right—shame on you!

🖤 *Louis Armstrong*

You're fed up, disgusted, confused, livid, devastated, and you can't take no more! Enough is enough already! You look a hot mess, and you feel even worse. You're eating nothing at all, or you're eating it all! Your thoughts keep finding themselves at destination *This is Some*

Bullshit! The game of love is over, and you just lost. Well, you didn't really lose, but that's your perception at the moment.

You poured your everything, and I mean your *e-ver-y-thing*, into him and your relationship. You gave much, much more than you ever took; you sacrificed when you really didn't have it to give; you compromised when you really didn't want to; you kissed his behind in order to feed his ego; you backed down when you should have stood up; you shut your mouth when you should have yelled at the top of your lungs; you cowered when you should have displayed genuine courage; you listened despite it being your turn to speak; you took less so he could have more; you laughed when you should have cried; you bent over backward and jumped through hoops so he'd be impressed; you cooked when you really wanted to be wined and

dined; you stayed in many miserable nights, hoping and praying that he'd come home at a decent
hour or at least call to check in, when you should
have hit the town and made some fun of your own
with the girls; you waited for him to change and do
better when you should have made peace with the
fact that he is who he is; you stayed after countless offenses and endured countless heartaches
when you should have made your exit stage left;
you were humble when you should have been
arrogant; you put out when you should have kept
it to yourself; you displayed patience despite
being worn out; you negotiated even when you
had nothing left to barter: you accepted being tolerated when you really needed to be loved and
adored; you were accommodating when you
should have been unaccommodating; you held
on to foolish hope and foolish pride when you

should have thrown in the towel rounds ago; you embraced fear—the fear of the unknown, the fear of not finding anyone better, the fear of not finding anyone at all—when you should have embraced your strength and exercised your faith; you settled when you should have made and stood by your demands; you held on to Relationship Nonsense when you should have turned it loose.

Should have, would have, could have, but *didn't*—until now. Now you are *really* ready to put yourself first. You are really ready to take your joy, your peace of mind, your strength, your power, and your life back!

In other words...*Boy Bye!*

2

Allow Me to Tell You Why I'm Done!

People show you who you want them to be until they have no choice but to show you who they really are.

♥ R. Hall

Scenario One:

He Was a Creeper!

Mr. Man was a repeat offender. Some female was *always* texting, emailing, calling, tweeting, instagraming, or hitting him up on Facebook. He was *always* texting, emailing, calling, tweeting, instagraming, or hitting some female up on Facebook. You stopped trusting and believing in him many moons ago. You knew he'd been with other women sexually, emotionally, and at times both sexually and emotionally. You knew it, and everybody else knew it too. He *stayed* in the streets. You constantly felt he was:

1. Being misleading about who he was *really* chatting it up with.

2. Withholding information about who he was *really* keeping time with.

3. Lying about where he was *really* located (Shawn's house or *Shawna's* house?).

Your self-esteem was on empty. And it was not because you weren't (and still are) an amazing woman, but because you didn't realize that his infidelity had absolutely nothing to do with you. Monogamy just isn't *his* thing. Commitment just isn't *his* thing. Being a one-woman man? It's just not *his* thing. Some men are just cheaters, wanderers, field-players, two-timers (three-and four-timers). You couldn't change that about him.

No matter how big and perky your boobs are; no matter how fat your backside is; no matter how toned the back of your legs look; no matter how many Kegel exercises you perform; no matter how fly your hair is styled; no matter how curvaceous your hips look in those skinny jeans; no matter how many weekly manicures and pedicures you get; no matter how well you think you put it down; no matter how well you can burn in the kitchen; no matter how spotless you keep your home; no matter how flawless that MAC makeup looks on your face; no matter how trim you keep your womanly bush; no matter how many football games you silently endure; no matter how smart you are; no matter how sweet you are; no matter how thoughtful, caring, and kind you are; no matter how hard you try to be a crazy, sexy, cool chick because you *heard* men love crazy, sexy, cool chicks, you still cannot change the ways of a cheating man.

None of your special talents or physical attributes could have affected the outcome of him being a faithless man, because his tricky ways were not about you. You tried it all, in concerted effort, to get him to put his bag of tricks down. Yet he still remained a repeat offender. So now you are done—*really* done this time—with being cheated on (aka disrespected, taken for granted, played, made a fool of, and not taken seriously). You didn't have the power to stop him from being a cheating man, but you absolutely possessed (and possess) the power to stop him from being a man who cheats on you. That power was exercised by your timely, or maybe not-so-timely, exit.

Scenario Two:

I'm Nobody's Good-Enough Girl!

He had you at hello. He was charming, easy-going, and not bad on the eyes. He was barrels of fun. He made you laugh, and laugh hard. He had a good job, good credit, and a good head on his shoulders. You wanted to believe your frog-kissing days were over. You were looking forward to going the distance with him. You loved him *so* much—and you felt he loved you too. But as the years slipped away, you started to wonder if your love for him was a tad bit stronger than his love for you. This wondering was forced to a head when you took an honest and thorough assessment of the sacrifices you were willing but he was unwilling to make and the fears you were willing to face in the Battle of Love, only to discover that you were fighting all alone (fighting all alone, fighting all alone, looking like a fool, because you're fighting all alone).

Mr. Man knew that you wanted to be married (by one or two years into the relationship). You remained consistent and unwavering in expressing your desires and expectations. He spoke and presented himself as if you were both on the same page, as if you both had mutual desires. But there was a dilemma on the horizon. His actions failed to coordinate with his impressive, get-your-hopes-up-all-high talk. Inevitably, you were burdened with the task of accepting that you were being taken for and treated as a Good-Enough Girl.

Good-Enough Girl: a female who is good enough to kick it with, good enough to sleep with, good enough to date *indefinitely*, good enough to shack with, but not *quite* good enough to marry.

He wanted married-man benefits but was only willing to pay single-man dues. Mr. Man wanted *a lot* from you: encouragement when he was discouraged, sex on a frequent basis, daily home-cooked meals, laundered and ironed clothes, shuttle service to and from the airport when he had to travel, peace and quiet when he didn't feel like talking, clean living quarters when he hadn't washed a single dish, space when he was feeling crowded, understanding when he was feeling confused, self-esteem boosters when his self-esteem was on low, to feel intelligent when his decisions didn't make an ounce of sense, his behind kissed when he should've been kissing yours, to be coddled when he was sick, the voids that couldn't be filled by the "homies" filled by you, the attention that he at times neglected to give, the adoration and respect that he at times neglected to show. *Wow!* That's a whole lot to receive while ONLY paying poor-single-man fees.

Marriage and commitment are just too serious, too heavy, for some men. And some men can afford the luxury of "keeping it light," particularly when they can get all of the previously mentioned high-end relationship merchandise at Filene's Basement bargain prices.

Men, Marriage, and Maybe's

♥Maybe he just wanted to ride the I'm-not-married-but-I-sure-get-all-the-perks-of-being-married gravy train until the wheels fell off (and then hop on someone else's gravy train).

♥Maybe he wasn't feeling marriage at the moment (he just wasn't ready for a serious commitment).

♥Maybe he wasn't feeling marriage with *you* (he just wasn't *that* into you).

♥Maybe he just wasn't feeling marriage period. Not yesterday, not today, not *ever* (he's just not the marrying type)!

You devoted time that could never be replaced and energy that could never be rejuvenated into trying to convince him that you were The One. You desperately wanted him to see, recognize, and acknowledge your It Girl quality. His inability—crooked vision and twisted thinking—to see, recognize, and acknowledge your amazingness didn't make you any less of an It Girl. It just positioned you as not the It Girl for *him*. And because you're the settling-down, wanting-to-get-married, not-wanting-to-be-a-fornicator, opposed-to-shacking-up, and liking-to-have-some-babies-one-day type of woman, he wasn't The One for you. He was unwilling to straighten up, fly right, and "put a ring on it," leaving you with the only option of exiting stage left.

You tried it all—bedroom tricks, securing the recipes for his favorite dishes, practicing the art of keeping your big mouth shut because men don't like nags, and more—to prove to this man that you were worthy of being escorted down that long, narrow aisle, handed off to him, and kissed in front of a church full of folk. You gave the relationship everything you had and were genuinely the best woman you could have possibly been for him— you were honest; you never cheated; you were caring and supportive; you made sacrifices; and you loved him with your entire being. But he *still* opted out. You could not have possibly done anything more to impress Old Boy. It didn't make an ounce of sense, for you're a beautiful person inside and out. You have a sense of humor; you have kitchen skills; you're not one of those psycho chicks; you go to church (most Sundays); you're not an In-the-Streets Girl; you're independent (which kept you out of his pockets); and you mesh well in social settings. Your list of pros can go on and on and on... to the next worthy and appreciative suitor.

It *finally* registered for you:

1. This man is NOT going to marry me!
2. This man probably had NO intentions of marrying me...ever!

The gig was up, and his joy riding was O-V-E-R...*over!* You concluded to be done—really done this time—with being strung along like a shiny tin can attached to a white, braided string, being yanked and jerked every which way down a newly-paved, brick road.

Sidebar: For many thirty-and-some-change ladies, throwing in the towel at this point may appear way too scary to handle. Scared E. Cat thoughts try to take over your mind.

Scared E. Cat Thoughts

1. Who is going to take care of me if I leave?

2. What if I wait just a little while longer?

3. I don't want to start all over again!

4. I can't leave now! I've invested too much time.

5. I'm too old.

6. What if I can't find anyone better?

7. What if I can't find anyone else at all?

8. What if he is the best I can do?

9. Nobody else is going to want me.

10. Isn't it better to have a man (even if I am settling) than to have no man at all?

The One Thought that Trumps ALL Scared E. Cat Thoughts

1. *Are you crazy?* Settling and operating out of fear is *not* sexy, *not* cool, *not* hot, *not* smart, *not* ever! Nothing about you says you have to accept settling for less.

My former barber, a gentleman from the Old School, told me as he was grooming the sides and the back of my short cut, "You can *still* find a good man…even at forty." You may not see the redeeming qualities of this statement initially. Who in the you-know-what wants to wait until they are forty to find their Mr. Good Man? But there *is* redemption in this statement. There is no expiration date stamped on your upper right shoulder. You don't expire or become less of anything—less beautiful, less intelligent, less sexy, less appealing, less worthy—because you are no longer a twenty something. You don't have to hold on for dear life to Relationship Nonsense just because your birthday cake has an additional candle sticking out of it. Sure, it may require some patience in waiting for a Mr. Good Man to make himself known. But in the interim, isn't it comforting to know that:

1. You're not selling yourself short any longer?

2. You're not being used up until you have nothing left to give?

3. You had more power and guts than you thought you had?

4. You pulled the plug on being treated as a Good-Enough Girl?

5. You walked away gracefully with your dignity still (somewhat) intact, as opposed to staying and begging and pleading and hoping (with your fingers and toes crossed) for the day when you've worn him down long enough to successfully *drag* him down the aisle?

Scenario Three:

He Wanted to Have

His Cake and Eat It Too!

You found yourself in a very tricky situation. He was beautiful, charming, and he had the most decadent, flawless, chocolate-brown skin you'd ever seen in your life. He was tall. He was sexy. Mr. Dark-'n-Lovely looked good with his waves dipped, his hair cut low, or with a bald head. He held the most interesting conversations and could make you laugh even when you didn't want to. He was a go-getter, and he knew how to make things happen. He was feeling you and you liked being felt. He made you feel beautiful. He was everything you've imagined your entire life a man should be. Mr. Man was just *like that*; Idris "Fine-As-I-Don't-Know-What" Elba *like that*, Boris "Too-Beautiful-for-Words" Kodjoe *like that*, Lance "Looking-Lovely" Gross *like that,* Denzel "Cool-As-An-Ice-Cube" Washington *like that*, President Barack "Smooth-Operator" Obama *like that*. He was just *like that!* He had endless flavor and indescribable swag…and his wife (or girlfriend) agreed.

Maybe you knew he was married or involved before you started dealing with him, maybe you didn't. But in all honesty, at the time, it would not have even mattered because you were already in way too deep. Mr. Dark-'n-Lovely had you thinking his wife or main lady was lame in bed or that she'd let herself go, that there was no longer any chemistry between them or that she no longer appreciated him, that for whatever reason(s) he couldn't stand her. He really had you under the impression that one day (one of these good old days) he was going to leave Mrs. Lame, Mrs. Annoying, Mrs. Mundane, Mrs. Let-Herself-Go, Mrs. Irks-the-Hell-Out-of-Me to be with *you* — Ms. Spicy, Ms. Delightful, Ms. Excitement, Ms. Sexy-As-Hell, Ms. Laid-Back.

Mr. Dark-'n-Lovely charmed you into thinking you were everything his wife or girlfriend was not, everything she could *never* be. In the beginning, you were hopeful and trusting enough to believe in him. But the question had to be asked and then examined: If Mrs. Lady was *so* lame, *so* humdrum, *so* annoying, such a you-know-what, and he was legitimately unhappy, why did he fail to sever ties with her prior to making your acquaintance? If she was *so* lame, *so* humdrum, *so* annoying, such a you-know-what, and he was *so* unhappy with her, why did he need your assistance, your convincing, and your encouragement to design his plan of escape? Why did he need you to aid and counsel him in making a decision involving his happiness versus his *alleged* misery?

More likely than not, Mr. Dark-'n-Lovely had no intention of abandoning his "miserable" life with The Missus to be with you (which has been made apparent by the fact that he's still with her). He selfishly used up a significant portion of your time and your energy (it required a great deal of time and energy to listen to all of his whining and complaining about her; it required a great deal of time and energy to try to convince him that you're the one he should *really* be with). Even if he was genuinely miserable with his wife or girlfriend…oh well. Those were personal concerns that should have never concerned you. His misery is *his* problem. How dare he try to make (or successfully make) his problems your problems as if you didn't have enough problems—the bills are due, the toilet's leaking, the car is making a strange sound, and your boss is hounding you—of your own.

Initially, you tried tirelessly to be that bright spot in his day. You provided listening ears for his moaning and groaning, sore shoulders for him to lean on, an open mind that was willing to entertain sexual fantasies Mrs. Lame allegedly would never entertain. You provided a "keeping it simple" relationship, because Mr. Man didn't want to do "complicated" with Ms. Spicy, Ms. Delightful, Ms. Excitement, Ms. Sexy-As-Hell, and Ms. Laid Back. You also provided a welcoming, cozy home environment that afforded him the pleasure of just "being easy," home-cooked meals because allegedly Mrs. Annoying didn't cook for him anymore, and whatever else you could think of that would expedite the process of him leaving her for good and being with you forever.

She—The Missus—could be compared to the educational (at times routine but always necessary) parts of the school day; the reading, mathematics, writing, social studies, science, and health. She was like the portion of the school day that actually requires the application of effort and hard work; the portion of the instructional day that demands dedication and commitment. You, Miss Lady, were like the fun but brief portions of the instructional day— lunch, recess, and PE. Not much effort or commitment required to enjoy and ace lunch, recess, or PE. But PE, recess, and lunch are only temporary breaks and relief from the real deal. What happens when the sounds of the lunch and recess bells are heard? You take your tail right back to class and you get real again. You jump right back into

that reading, mathematics, writing, social studies, science, or health textbook, and playtime is
O-V-E-R...*over!*

And this was the nature of your relationship
with him. You provided him with temporary breaks
and relief from his responsibilities. But after an
enjoyable but short-lived time with you, at the
sound of the bell (his wife or main-girl beckoning),
he always sashayed his behind right back to his
classroom (his life with his wife or main girl) and
left you feeling as deserted, empty, and lonely as a
recess playground with zero children sliding down
the slides, swinging on the swings, bouncing the
bouncy balls, climbing across the monkey bars,
playing tag, jump-roping, or laughing with delight
on it.

You finally grew physically exhausted, spiritually
weary, and emotionally drained from playing the

game with him. You tired of being his plaything, his girl on the side, his undercover and behind-closed-doors "boo." You yearned for much more out of the relationship. You deserved much more than he had or was willing to offer. As a result, you decided it was way past due to invest the energy, care, and love once reserved for him into something more profitable—physically, spiritually, and emotionally profitable. And hopefully you escaped the secret relationship without his wife or main girl whacking the "Maybe She's Born with It" Maybelline right off of your face.

Scenario Four:

I Will Not Settle for Less Than I'm Worth!

Your relationship was miles from Peachy Street. From day one, things regarding your involvement could not have possibly been rated peachy, not even on a rating curve. Despite the poor and painfully honest rating of your relationship, you decided to remain a factor in the You + Him= Under-Performing Relationship equation for undoubtedly longer (and possibly *way* longer) than suggested. You gave him a pass to treat you in a manner that, for lack of a better term, *sucked*. He lied constantly; you stayed with him. He stayed in the streets nightly (with only God knows who), despite your ineffective protests; you stayed with him. He showed you very little, if any, attention, affection, and adoration, despite your begging and pleading for it; still…you stayed. His communications with you were disrespectful and degrading; but still you stayed. His displays of genuine love and care were non-existent; yet still…you stayed.

You adopted the philosophy that having a man who treats you in a lousy manner was better than not having a man at all. You bought into the belief that holding on to a man who treats you poorly was better than being alone. And as a result, settling took place. You settled for bottom of the barrel treatment even though you deserved the royal treatment (red carpet rolled out and all). You settled for little to no communication despite your being born to "chat it up" and express yourself.

You settled for dull and boring when you really craved spontaneity and excitement. You settled for gift-less Valentine's Days when you yearned for romantic cards, red roses, rich chocolates, and rare pieces of jewelry. You settled for simply being tolerated when you were really worth appreciation and celebration. You settled for simply having an invitation to the relationship party despite being the guest of honor. You settled for tenth and eleventh player compensation despite being the LeBron James, the Paul George, the D-Wade, the Kevin Garnett, the Chris Paul, and the Kevin Durant on the court of your relationship.

The Bad News: It feels "sucky" admitting that we've sold ourselves short; that we didn't set greater demands for how we're to be regarded and treated in our relationships.

The Best News: Thankfully you realized that you deserve and should receive more from your relationship(s). You made the decision to govern yourself accordingly. And as a result you pulled the plug on Operation Settling for Less.

Scenario Five:

Married...But

Miserably Just Won't Do!

You were eagerly anticipating your special day—the day you've been not-so-patiently waiting for practically your entire life! The relationship had its ups and its downs, and in some instances its *way* ups and its *way* downs. But none of that mattered because you were super excited about being initiated into The Married Woman's Club. You selected the most perfect gown for your special day. It was simply exquisite, with classic lace and beaded detailing. You managed to narrow the bridesmaid's roster to only six of your closest and dearest friends. The wedding colors—lavender, silver, and white—were selected what seemed ages ago. Color coordinated M&M favors were ready for distribution, and your gift pouch was looking forward to generous deposits—chi-ching. Your smile had more sparkle than the four-carat, princess-cut, platinum-band ring you sported on your perfectly manicured and polished left hand, fourth finger. The bachelorette party went down (and what happened at your "bachee" shall forever remain there).

Hubby looked so handsome and dapper in his well-fitted, black tuxedo with the coordinating lavender accessories, his fresh-cut, crisp lineup, and clean-shaven face (and he smelled good too). You looked stunning in your white gown, perfectly polished face, and perfectly pinned-up hair. You heard statements like, "The ceremony was so beautiful," "You look like a princess," "Your dress is lovely," "What a beautiful couple", and

"Congratulations" over and over. And you enjoyed every single second of it.

Your reception was one of the best parties ever! There were signature drinks served, an open bar, and plenty of designated drivers on deck; delicious foods your guests couldn't get enough of; old-school throwbacks and new school tunes entertained your guests the entire evening (they cupid shuffled, wobbled, and shook their tail feathers until being forced to leave the reception hall). The fellas didn't make a huge fuss over catching your garter belt. But your girlfriend, who flew in from New York, was determined to out catch all the other single ladies in attendance for your perfectly arranged bouquet. After all the stomach stuffing, wine tasting, cupcake devouring, glass tapping, shoe changing, garter belt avoiding, bouquet catching, line dancing, picture posing, chatting, and grinning, you and hubby were honeymoon bound.

Shortly after your arrival back to the States, someone decides to start showing off. Guess who? Your new husband. He's not meeting married man expectations at all. He likes to roam the streets with Mike and them as if he's still a single-man pass holder. He has way too many Facebook friends and Twitter followers (long-hair-having, sparkling-teeth-grinning, and eyelash-batting friends and followers). He's not taking you out on date nights anymore. His communication with you has fallen off…way off. You keep catching him in shady truths causing you to grow increasingly suspicious of him. You've reviewed his phone records only to discover unsettling and incriminating pieces of information. He's withdrawn emotionally; he's withdrawn physically. He acts as if he just doesn't care anymore. The sound of your voice irks the hell out of him; the sound of his voice irks the hell out of you. He spends more time out of the home than in it, and when he is home, he's *not* home. He's like the stranger Tamia sang about in "Stranger in My House."

This is not what you signed up for. He used to make you feel as if you were the most beautiful woman in the world, and now he has you feeling more like a burden and a nuisance; like a sharp, pointy tack stuck in the left side of one of his behind cheeks. You used to feel like the two of you had a friendship, and now he barely seems to enjoy speaking with or even being in the same room as you. The compliments he used to give have silenced, and harsh critiques are now their substitutes. Intimate pillow talk has been swapped for the sounds of crickets outside your bedroom window. Affectionate cuddling has been replaced by brushing against oversized pillows purposely positioned to create barriers between the two of you. You suggested counseling on numerous occasions, and he's refused counseling… on numerous occasions. Your patience has worn thin; your strength has waned; your feelings have been crushed to unfixable pieces, and your spirit is shattered. You're talked out, cried out, fussed out, prayed out, emotionally wiped out, about to physically pass out, and now you want O-U-T… out.

Note: You may have had issues with him prior to saying "I do." But you didn't give those issues their due attention, because you really wanted to be married, and you were probably hoping he'd automatically transform into the man you so desperately dreamed your dream husband would be. Distinguishing the dream from the reality has proven to be very disheartening.

Maybe his behavior was *totally* new, *totally* bizarre, and *totally* shocking. The responsibilities of marriage, a personal life crisis, or feelings of complete confusion could have been the cause for the changes in his behavior. You kept asking yourself, "Who is this man, and what has he done with my husband? What has he done with my friend?" Whether his behavior was somewhat expected or had you completely dazed, you put in tireless days, nights, weeks, months, and years trying to get right with a husband who was no longer interested in honoring his commitment to his wife; a husband, who somewhere along the way, developed a change of heart but didn't have the courage to admit it.

He opted, instead, to mask his genuine feelings, to pounce on you emotionally, to be as mean and as crappy as possible, to be as inconsiderate and insensitive as imaginable, to be unbelievably selfish, and to chip away, bit by bit, at your spirit and your well-being. Maybe he was hoping for the day that you'd finally declare, "Oh, hell no. Enough is enough," and call it off—because if you ended it he wouldn't look like the bad guy. He wouldn't look like the guy who abandoned his marriage and left it shipwrecked. But he *is* the guy who abandoned his marriage (without doing his due diligence in trying to make it work). He *is* the guy who disrespectfully ditched a friendship. He *is* the guy who totally disregarded his teammate's feelings, wants, and needs. He *is* the guy who didn't keep his end of the bargain. He *is* the guy whose cowardice made life much more miserable for you than it needed to be. He *is* the guy who failed to remember how loyalty and allegiance work. He didn't walk away physically, but he walked away in every other manner possible.

Your marriage and your desire to make it work cost you damn near everything you had of true value. You wrote checks from your Joy, Peace of Mind, Rest-Filled Nights, and Self-Esteem accounts to finance your time with him. You woke up one day and declared NO MORE. You had absolutely nothing more to invest in him and your marriage. You were physically, emotionally, and spiritually bankrupt. And you declared it time to let go of the unhealthy marriage and re-up on all the things you were feeling depleted of.

In Closing

For whatever reason or combination of reasons, you're *finally* done—really done this time! You've made your decision—your grown-woman decision—and this time you are determined to stand by your decision. Parting ways is super tough. Picking up the pieces post parting-ways season is super tough. But you already knew that. That's more than likely why it took you so long to arrive at destination I'm Done For Real This Time. And although parting ways and picking up the post parting-ways pieces is tough…it's not impossible. You are beyond ready, more than determined, and highly equipped to put in the time and effort needed to:

1. Accept and grieve the loss of your relation-ship and all the hopes you had for it.

2. Pick yourself up, dust yourself off, and put one foot in front of the other in a more healthy and productive direction.

3. Reevaluate your relationship expectations, re-up on everything you've been depleted of, and re-build a happier, stronger, improved, and healthier you.

3

The Game Plan for Pushing Forward

There's a time for departure

even when there's no certain

place to go.

❧ Tennessee Williams

Step One:

Cry!

Weeping may endure for a night,

but joy cometh in the morning.

♥ **Psalms** 30:5

So it's officially over. And now it's time to release all your tears—tears of pain, tears of sadness, tears of disappointment, tears of frustration, tears of confusion, tears of anger, tears of devastation, tears of lost hope, and tears of fear. Take some time to pour your heart and eyeballs out, to scream until the glass shatters (if you need to; if you want to), to bust the windows out his car (NOT!). You more likely than not feel like committing a few acts of destruction. However, doing so will not assist you in the process of moving on in a healthy fashion; so try (real, real hard) not to entertain any destructive thoughts.

You're in a dark, sad place. Your hair is a matted mess. Sunlight hasn't kissed your swollen (from crying) face in days. Fresh air hasn't flown up your congested nostrils in days. Fresh hot water hasn't splashed any of your curves in days. Deodorant hasn't met your armpits in days. A flat iron hasn't caressed your limp tresses in days. Lip gloss hasn't connected with your lips in days. Mascara hasn't extended your lashes in days. And a "hot girl" outfit hasn't hugged your body…in days.

The Bad News: You stink, you look a hot mess, and you don't even care.

The Good News: You have a seven-day pass to stay in this dark, sad, neglectful (neglecting to be a diva) place.

The only thing you are truly committed to doing in the moment is crying. So cry then. Let it all out. You've been through a lot and it hurts. However, you still have to feed your body in between your crying splurges. Throw on a pair of rainy-day sweats, an oversized T-shirt, your I'm-having-a-bad-hair-day baseball cap, and your tinted shades. You only need to muster up enough energy to make it to your local grocery store for fridge, freezer, and cabinet-stocking purposes. Load up on all of your favorite foods and tasty treats: rotisserie chicken, turkey wings, barbeque wings, chips and dip, blueberry muffins, butter pecan ice cream, frozen pizza, caramel popcorn—whatever you like. You have a temporary pass to indulge yourself (you'll be back into a fitness regimen soon enough). For now, cry and eat, eat and cry, and cry and eat some more. Snuggle up with your most favorite cozy comforter and puffy pillows. Keep several boxes of Kleenex—the extra, extra soft Kleenex that contains aloe vera—by your bedside, or couch side, or by your bedside *and* couch side for your many crying splurges.

Note: *If you get one of the generic tissue brands, under your nose and under your eyes will become extremely raw and extremely sore (ouch!) after all the wiping and patting of your tears and the blowing of your nose.*

You may want to recruit close friends and family to vent to during your first post-breakup week. Your pass also allows you approximately one week to vent, host a breakup talk-a-thon, and bash ex-boo, which will ultimately lead to even more crying. However, after the allotted time is up, you will not continue to breathe additional life into your breakup and the circumstances surrounding it. This is very tough to do. As women, and I'm just being honest, we tend to be attracted to drama at times. And there is nothing more drama filled, for a woman, than a breakup. Our anger, our pain, our thoughts, our repeated conversations about how "he did me so wrong" extends breakup drama's shelf life far longer than it needs to be extended.

A conscious decision has to be made to talk your breakup story out, then let the story go, so you can move forward and create new stories (void of drama) to talk about. Hopefully this conscious decision is made sooner rather than later. But while you're crying your heart, your eyeballs, and your story out, remember and find comfort in knowing that God wipes away the tears of all his children. Weeping will endure for the night, or in this case a whole bunch of nights, but joy and sunshine will definitely be back for you.

Step Two:

Let Go So You Can Move On!

Sometimes it takes more strength to let go than it does to hold on.

💜 *Pastor Lee P. Washington*

Now that you've cried a river, gained an extra pound or two, and concluded the "he did me so wrong" talk-a-thon, you're ready to move on to step two. It's time to remove all (or at least most) items from your apartment, condo, or home that remind you of Mr. Ex. Items to be removed from your space include (but are not limited to) his basketball sneakers, Timberland boots, Kenneth Cole casuals, Nike sneaker boots, short-sleeve polo shirts, long-sleeve button down shirts, Calvin Klein dress shirts, hooded sweat shirts, frat tees, college tees, raggedy tees, funky tees, football jerseys, work slacks, distressed jeans, khakis, solid-colored ties, striped ties, socks with holes in them, socks without holes in them, Hanes boxers, Fruit of the Loom briefs, fitted baseball caps, wave caps, Nautica watches, Versace cologne, CDs, DVDs, magazines, pictures, and any other item that needs an eviction notice.

Note: *Neither Mr. Ex nor his memory-filled belongings are paying storage fees so Boy Bye! to them.*

Even the charming and sentimental gifts he's given you over the years may have to find the nearest exit. You may think getting rid of his gifts is unnecessary, but holding on to these items can potentially prolong your stay in a dark, sad place, hoping against all hope that the outcome could have been different. So the pearl earrings, the Tiffany heart-shaped necklace, the silver pearl bracelet, the DKNY watch with the white face, the New Balance workout sneakers, the Coach handbag, the Versace Bright Crystal and Vera Wang perfume, and other gifts that hold the potential to keep you trapped in the past, inducing tear-filled memories of yesterday (or yester-was), should kindly be excused. You need space from him and all things that are reminders of him.

You can place all of his belongings and gifts into containers of your choosing: packing boxes, plastic containers with lids, or a crowd favorite—trash bags. Once the items have been gathered and packed, rid your space of them as you choose fit.

Here are just a few suggestions:

1. Return everything back to Mr. Ex (sans cutting, shredding, burning, or bleaching). Imagine the expression on his face when he arrives home, after a long, hard day of work, only to be greeted by trash bags, filled to capacity, with all of his items, that you've kindly set free. #Priceless.

   Note: If you'd rather not waste your gas (your high-priced gas) driving all the way from your place to his place and back to your place again, you can arrange to meet him at a location of your choosing so he can retrieve his belongings. A neutral, public pick-up location will help to ensure a brief and civil exchange. If he's to come to your place, consider leaving temporarily and having a friend or family member present to oversee the pick-up process. This will help to avoid any lengthy and unnecessary exchanges between the two of you.

2. Donate his items to a charity, organization, or shelter of your choice.

3. Sell his items on EBay, Craigslist, or to a consignment shop. (Why not put a little extra cash in your pocket?)

Note: *Prior to donating or selling any of the ex's items, extend him the courtesy of securing his belongings (in a timely fashion of course). It's only fair.*

Clearing out can be physically and emotionally draining, but for your well-being, it's worth it. You should now have living quarters absent of Mr. Man and Mr. Man's belongings. Congratulations! You're well on your way to pushing forward.

Step Three:

Operation Upgrade

I'm just sayin' you could do better.

♥ ***Drake***

It's time to replace, also known as upgrade, a gift (or two) that Mr. Ex gave you...before he was Mr. Ex. In the interest of being financially responsible, don't try to replace all of his gifts at one time. We definitely don't want to slip into a pool of debt trying to get over him. He's already, directly or indirectly, intentionally or unintentionally, voluntarily or involuntarily, caused enough pain as is.

Operation Upgrade: You've returned, sold, or donated the silver-plated, white-faced watch Mr. Ex bought you for your thirty-first birthday. Naturally, you want, deserve, and need another one. Your task is to find and purchase a new watch that's even more beautiful, even more elegant, even more chic, even more ladylike, and has even more character than the one presented to you by Mr. Ex. Every time you look, or even glance, at your new and upgraded watch (or whatever you decide to upgrade—a bracelet, necklace, earrings), rest assured that your upgraded Knight is eagerly searching for you. And just like your new watch, bracelet, necklace, or earrings he'll look even better on you too (wink). #ComfortingToKnow

If, for whatever odd reason, you happened to be involved with a person who was too cheap, too stingy, or too silly to believe in gift giving, then you're actually in financial luck. Operation Upgrade will hardly break the bank for you. It's very easy to upgrade from absolutely, positively close to nothing. Stop by your local florist (or your local grocery store's flower department), and buy yourself a beautiful bouquet of simply gorgeous and delicious-smelling flowers. You may find yourself delighting in your flower bouquet so much so that you continue purchasing the weekly or biweekly plant-life treat. The beauty and comforting smells of your bouquets can serve as charming reminders that your Prince Charming exists, that he's diligently searching, and that he's determined to find his treasure—you.

Step Four:

Shut It Down!

~·~·~

Don't talk to me.

💙 *Unknown*

You're not strong enough to communicate with him right now. It'll be way too easy for Mr. Ex to put you back under his love spell. He'll charm you right out of your leisure suit and smooth-talk you right out of your casual day underwear. As women, for some strange reason, we feel compelled to accept our former boo's fifty thousand post-breakup phone calls; we feel compelled to respond to each and every one of his fifty thousand post-breakup text messages; we feel compelled to accept his "I'm sincere *this* time" apology. This isn't the first time you've been at intersection "I'll Do Better This Time I Promise" with Mr. Ex. But if you stand by your grown-woman decision to be treated in a more dignified manner, it can be the last.

Most times, when the past calls, texts, e-mails, Facebooks, or tweets, it usually has absolutely nothing new to talk about. You're not obligated to entertain him simply because he's reaching out, with urgency, to communicate. And why is he reaching out with such urgency now that you've ended the relationship (for real this time)? Why didn't he care enough to make things work while your relation-ship was in bloom? Why didn't he care enough to provide thorough answers to your many questions upon immediate delivery while you were still with him? Why didn't he care enough to design and comply with a Behavior Improvement Plan before your patience ran out?

He's behaving as if it's so pressing now only because he's trying to satisfy his ego. Mr. Ex has already shown you with his actions that you two are on different pages of the book (you may even be reading two totally different books with two totally different themes). You want one thing. He's demonstrated wanting something totally different. And because you've ended the relationship and you're no longer, in his mind, one of his possessions, his ego has been challenged and threatened. The idea of you leaving him, giving time and attention to someone or something other than him, is viewed as a failure. His ego is terribly threatened by failure. You've put him in a position where he feels pressured to win (again). If he wins—convinces, charms, or cons another chance out of you—his ego is satisfied, and he gets to feel like he's "That Dude" again. (As I write this, I can't help but think that I sure wish I knew *then* what I know *now.*)

It's like a game or a sport for him. For you, it's not a game at all—it's real. It's your life! You must make your selection on how best to proceed based on the fact that you didn't arrive at destination This is Some Bullshit overnight. It took a lot of time, agony, tears, aches, pains, and frustration getting there. You've been through this with him before. This is a déjà vu moment. How you decide to handle this situation is crucial.

Selection One Comes With:

1. Giving in to his impromptu attempts at communication.

2. Allowing him to get your hopes up by telling you everything he's going to do differently, everything he's going to do better. (**Reminder:** He's had countless opportunities to modify his behavior in the past.)

3. Sleeping with him, and you mistaking the temporary and passionate thrill for his commitment to and undying love for you.

4. Desperately hoping that things will be different *this* time.

5. Ultimately him showing his behind and settling back into his same old, tired routine.

6. And now you're livid because deep down (and maybe not so deep down), you knew this would be the end result.

Note: You can call it love, or you can call it insanity — doing the same thing over and over and over, but *expecting different results, only to continue getting the same old same old.*

Selection Two Comes With:

1. Telling him to delete your phone number when he calls. (He most likely won't delete your number, but you'll feel so empowered by simply saying, "Delete my number, and thank you very kindly, sir.")

2. Ignoring his future phone calls and text messages (because he has not deleted your number) that have the underlying purpose of persuading you out of your pink panties.

3. Letting him know with your words AND your actions that he's just been announced the

loser of the game he enjoys playing so well, because you're over it. #OverItDotCom

With Selection Two, it is made crystal clear that you are no longer willing to be taken around and around on his roller-coaster ride to NOWHERE! Choosing Selection Two is your way of effectively saying, "Stop this roller-coaster ride right here and right now! I'm getting off, sir. You are more than welcome to keep riding (and going around and around). Just not with me."

Step Five:

Accept and Find the

Blessing in It Being Over

Know that everything is in perfect order whether you understand it or not.

♥ Guy Finley

You've cried, cleared out, and shut down communication, but it still hurts. His unwillingness to fully reciprocate the love, time, and care you poured into him feels more painful than a stinging slap to the face or a forceful, air-stealing punch to the stomach. His overall relationship performance clearly demonstrated that he wasn't *that* into you; not into you enough to establish a culture of balance and reciprocity in your relationship.

You couldn't change what he was willing to give or commit. And that's not to be interpreted as a poor reflection of you. You simply couldn't change him; you couldn't coerce him into loving, adoring, or committing to you (and nor should you have had to). Trying to force love is like trying to squeeze a size-eight, "I-don't-think-you're-ready-for-this-jelly" form into a size-two pair of True Religion skinny jeans—what an uncomfortable, painful, humiliating, sloppy, disaster of a mess. The best thing to do now is to accept that he failed to really see and benefit from the beauty in you (and that's on him). The next best thing to do is to accept that he just wasn't *that* into you, for reasons far beyond your control.

He Just Wasn't That Into You Situations

Situation One: Maybe he didn't want to commit to being in a relationship with you. He just wasn't *that* into you; not enough to make a commitment.

Situation Two: Maybe he didn't spoil, adore, and provide you with all the love, care, and security you needed. He just wasn't *that* into you; not enough to dedicate all the time, effort, and energy required to make you feel loved and cared for.

Situation Three: Maybe he strung you along, procrastinated, and didn't feel compelled to "put a ring on it." He just wasn't *that* into you; not enough to change his introduction of you from "This is my girl

(my Good-Enough Girl),_____."
                              [insert your name here]

to "This is my wife, Mrs. _____."
                              [insert his last name here]

Sidebar: It's easy, convenient, and ego-satisfying

to make excuses for men and "mighty marriage."

Examples of excuses women fool themselves into

temporarily believing when it comes to men and

marriage include, but are not limited to:

1. He hasn't asked me to marry him after eight

    years of dating and playing house because

    he doesn't have the money right now. (Quick

    Fix: Justice of the Peace)

2. He's just not where he wants to be in life

    right now. (How long should your life be put

on hold waiting for him to arrive at where he thinks he wants to be?)

3. He's afraid of marriage, so I should be more patient with him. (Have you not already been patient?)

Men really are not that complicated, I've come to learn. If they want to do something, they do it. If they don't want to do something, they don't do it. Pretty plain. Pretty simple.

Note: *Please, please, please don't interpret his demonstration of not being that into you as indication or confirmation that you're not good enough, that you're less than, or that you're not worthy of real love. You are more than amazing and it's too bad, too sad for him that he failed to thoroughly see you and that he's no longer able to take advantage of your amazingness! Thankfully the right* *gentleman, a deserving gentleman, will appreciate you for the amazing woman you truly are.*

Acceptance helps you move on. When I have to accept things, events, and circumstances I'm not particularly pleased with, I repeat this saying as many times as needed: It is what it is, and it's not what it can't be.

Personal Story: It was a sunny and pleasant August Saturday in Washington, DC. The year was 2007. A dear friend would be kissing her last first kiss shortly after hearing and saying "I do." We were all bridesmaids: Chantal, Dawn, Shatikwa, and I. As we lined up alongside the church, prior to making our grand entrance for the wedding ceremony, tiny, cold, wet droplets started descending from the sky. Yes! The sky started sprinkling on our freshly relaxed and styled hairdos, threat-ening to transform those styles from tame and attractive hair into Lord-have-mercy hair. Yes! The sky started sprinkling on our freshly beat faces, threatening to put skin that was less than flaw-less on blast. Yes! The sky started sprinkling on our lovely, strapless, mint-green satin (Or was it sateen?) bridesmaid's dresses, threatening to cre-ate unwanted wrinkling. Oh, yes! The sky started sprinkling, tempting curves barely concealed in strapless dresses to become publicly exposed, thus turning our friend's wedding into an episode of Bridesmaids Gone Wild.

Instinctively, we all started to complain: "Oh my goodness! My hair! I can't believe it's rain-ing!" The wedding coordinator, probably highly annoyed with our complaining, stated, very direct and calmly, "Ladies, yes, it's raining. But it is what it is." It didn't take long for us to realize that there was absolutely nothing we could do about changing the sky's desire to shower us on that particular day, at that particular moment. Could we force the sky to stop planting raindrops on us? Could we run back into the church and leave our dear friend bridesmaids-less on her special day? Absolutely not! We just had to accept it. We didn't like it, but we had to accept it. Those words—"it is what it is"—simply stated, helped me to put things into better perspective that day and for many days to follow. It helps me better grasp that I will experience unpleasant and unexpected events and circumstances that are totally out of my control that I won't like but that I'll plainly have to accept.

Note: *The ceremony was just lovely by the way. My friend married her soul mate and the sprinkles let up just enough to keep our hairdos intact, our blemishes hidden, and our bare curves out of view. No Bridesmaids Gone Wild fest that day.*

Another helpful saying that allows me to refocus and to put things into positive perspective is, "What's for me is for me; what's not for me is not for me." Is it fair to say he wasn't for you for whatever reason or reasons? Accepting so, as opposed to trying to calculate the whys, the why-nots, the maybes, and the what-ifs, will grant you the peace and freedom to move on. And at this stage, moving on may not be finding the next boo but rather moving on to simply being and feeling OK, moving on to putting yourself first again, moving on to holding your head high once again, moving on to accepting that things didn't work out because things weren't supposed to work out.

And Another Personal Story: Shortly after parting ways with my college sweetheart (more like sourheart), I met the sweetest guy. He was tall, had cocoa-brown skin, attended a neighboring college, held doors for me, paid for dates, and he bought me cute little gifts just because. He was absolutely perfect. But guess who wasn't ready to receive such a delightful blessing? *Me!* There was absolutely nothing more Jay could have possibly done to win me over, because he wasn't the issue—I was.

When relationships break down, we automatically feel as if we did something wrong or that we didn't do enough things right. Jay did everything right, but my silly behind was too busy boohoo-ing over a gentleman who will absolutely remain nameless, to truly appreciate and receive him. This may be the case for you now. You've done every-thing you could have possibly done for the sake of the relationship, but for reasons beyond your control, beyond your comprehension, he wasn't ready; he wasn't mentally or emotionally capable of truly and thoroughly appreciating and receiv-ing you as the blessing you intended to be, as the blessing you were more than ready and willing to be in his life. But that's a cross he'll have to carry, not you. You just have to come to terms with the fact that there's another chapter to be written in your story of love, one in which he's no longer a supporting character.

I was the best thing Jay never had. And me being so, I'm certain, afforded him the opportunity to meet someone who was willing and able to appreciate him the way he deserved to be appreciated. In this moment, your ex is the best thing you never had, which only gives you an opportunity to be the best thing your next boo will ever have. So for now, pour yourself a glass (or maybe two) of your favorite red or white wine and replay Beyoncé's song "Best Thing I Never Had" as many times as necessary. Things may not make much sense now, but in the days, weeks, months, and years to follow, all will be made clear. You'll see that you look even better in your future than you did in your past. He wasn't *that* into you, because he wasn't supposed to be *that* into you. Someone else has been created to be *that* into you. And that's your blessing…not your burden.

Step Six:

Pray! A LOT!

~~~~~

Pray, and let God worry.

♥ **Martin Luther**

You've been operating in whirlpool mode with all the crying, clearing out, upgrading, cutting off communication, and accepting that he wasn't supposed to be *that* into you. The storm is passing, somewhat. The silent (and not so silent) screams of rage and anger have toned down. Rage and anger are slowly moving on so space for sadness and disappointment can be made. Sadness and disappointment are not loud and active like rage and anger, but rather quiet and still. In these quiet and still moments, despite your journey of acceptance, you'll find yourself desperately feeling like you desperately need and want to cry out, "This is not fair! I didn't deserve this! I'm trying my hardest to be strong, but deep down I am still hurting. I don't understand why this is happening to me" or "I don't understand why this is happening to me *again*."

You're confused and hurt, also known as the perfect posture for prayer. Say whatever is on your mind to the one who sees all and knows all. Confess wholeheartedly that you are in dire need of some outside assistance with this life crisis (and YES! breakups always *feel* like a life crisis for a woman).

Humbly but boldly petition God for what you need—joy, strength, and comfort. If you want the sadness taken away, ask Him to give you joy like a river overflowing. If you want the strength to get out of bed and face the world, flashing a "fake it until you believe it" smile, ask Him to pump strength back into your fragile and emotionally-weak body. If you want to feel comforted and to feel His presence so you'll know that you have not been forsaken, ask Him to wrap his loving arms around you. God can and He will provide you with all the joy, all the strength, and all the comfort needed to accompany you on your journey through all the pain, through all the sadness, and through all the confusion.

Personal Story: I really thought that I was in a promising (let's-get-married, buy-a–house-together, take-care-of-the-dog, and *possibly*-make-a-baby-together promising) relationship. After the weeks rolled into months and the months rolled into years and the proposal to propose started to age and then rot, the light bulb in my head *finally* came on, and with it came the realization that this man does *not* want to marry me (not today and probably not tomorrow either).

With that realization, I learned a tough yet valuable lesson: It's *so* much harder to let go than it is to hold on at times. Letting go signifies taking a huge leap of faith, venturing into the unknown, and trusting God to keep you through it all. And although it was scary as hell to walk away at age thirty from a four-year relationship, I had to get like Nike and *just do it.* It was as if God was whispering (the kind of whispers that keep you up late at night, the kind of whispers that refuse to hush until you appease them, the kind of whispers that make you feel uncomfortable, the kind of whispers that you try to drown out with your own thoughts of denial) in my ear. And for a long while, I tried really hard to shush those whispers that were saying, "I have something different in mind for you. This relationship, as it currently stands, has run its course. It's now time for you to move on."

But, there were no prospects, or even potential prospects, within a fifty, seventy-five, or one-hundred-mile radius for me to explore the option of moving on with when I finally mustered up enough courage to make my grand exit, which in actuality wasn't so grand at all. I said something like, "I love you, and I want to be married one day, but not badly enough to drag you down the aisle. I'm inclined to believe you were being misleading when you indicated that you wanted to marry me and that an engagement was on the horizon.

You want the perks of being married, but you're unwilling to sacrifice the commitment required to be married. If you are not ready and willing to marry me after a four-year courtship today, then most likely you won't be ready tomorrow either. I'm done playing the wait-around game. There's nothing else I can possibly do to *persuade* you. And as a result, I think it's time we go our separate ways."

If you position all of the TVs and radios in your home to off, put your cell phone on silent, and make sure there's no water dripping from your kitchen sink, you'll have the speaks-more-than-volumes response I was the baffled recipient of receiving from said young man. So, not only was I thirty years old, but now I was thirty (almost thirty-one) years old…and single. (In the infamous words of Martin Lawrence..."Damn, Gina!") The way society tells it, I should have picked out my casket as well as the dress I wanted to be buried in right then and there.

I could have continued dating said young man. (By the way...I did receive a response two weeks later indicating that he didn't want things to end; he just wasn't ready for marriage.) I guess I could have been ecstatic about being good enough to be his Good-Enough Girl and explored that option for another, say, four or five years. But I opted to be obedient to God's will and trust Him instead.

In my anger, sadness, and confusion, I'd say to God, "I trusted you. Why did you set me up like this? Why are people allowed to enter my space, misrepresent themselves, and mislead me, leaving me all alone to pick up the fragmented emotional pieces and put my game face *back* on?" When I called on God, He answered. Not in a conventional manner. But I felt His presence comforting me; I felt my emotionally-weak body and my crushed spirit strengthening; I could feel the emotionally hefty luggage being removed from my arms so I could journey more freely. I could hear God saying, "I do love you. Always know that. I know what's best for you far better than you do. I'd never set you up. Don't ever stop trusting me. You look even better in your future than you did in your past." I heard Him, and I believed Him. And then something magical would happen. I would start to feel lighter. I would start to feel that everything *was* going to be OK. I would start to feel more and more OK with each day and with each prayer.

I shared all that just to say that God hears and answers our prayers. It may not be in a you'll-meet-your-Prince-Charming-tomorrow-at-the-Starbucks-at-approximately-three-o'clock-so-wear-your-most-flattering-outfit kind of way. He doesn't work on our time or on our schedules. But He always provides us with what we need—experiences, severed relationships, new relationships, trials, triumphs, disappointments, and victories—when we need it.

In addition to asking God to take the post-breakup anger, sadness, pain, and confusion away (or at least make it more manageable with each passing day), you may also want to consider praying for:

1. Clarity of thought.
2. Peace of mind.

3. The ability to forgive your ex for intentionally or unintentionally hurting you. And with the ability to forgive comes the ability to let the anger go. I came to a point where I was tired of being angry; tired of putting energy into being angry. Look, we all make mistakes. No one is perfect. I don't think my ex-boyfriend was intentionally trying to hurt me at all. I think there came a point where he couldn't avoid being honest with himself a second longer. This, in turn, naturally forced him to be honest with me (it was delayed honesty but honesty nonetheless). And although at the time I was crushed, I now appreciate the experience and his delayed honesty—which I'm confident, has spared me additional buckets of unnecessary tears and unwanted heartache in the long run.

4. The ability to forgive yourself, if needed, and to let things go. During my post-breakup period, I'd blame myself for not being smarter, for refusing to see the red flags, for giving much more benefit than doubt. I had to release myself and my ex-boyfriend from the emotional prison I had us both held captive in.

5. The ability to actively look for and find the good in good-bye. Sometimes the good in letting go is providing yourself with an opportunity to grow into a stronger, wiser, and more peaceful person.

Step Seven:

Laugh! A LOT!

~~~

What soap is to the body, laughter is to the

soul.

💜 *Yiddish proverb*

Now that you've cried your heart out, cleared your space out, ignored his attempts to put you back under his spell, accepted that he didn't have the capacity to give you what you wanted or what you needed, and assumed the posture of prayer position, it's finally time to invite laughter back into your life. Sometimes when we are down and out, we opt to just be alone. Being alone is an understandable pill to want to swallow at this time, but that pill is dangerous when taken in large dosages. While you're people-free and laughter-free, your mind will try to take you right back down Failed-Relationship Memory Lane. You're working on the acceptance piece, but you will still experience moments of heavy sadness. You'll start to feel sorry for yourself. Insane thoughts will try forcing their way into your mind. Some of those insane thoughts may include:

1. Nobody wants me.

2. I'm not desirable.

3. Everybody has a man but me; something must be wrong with me.

4. I should just call him and put myself out of my misery. (Self-inflicted misery is what you're in. Yes. You are genuinely sad about the breakup, but when you entertain thoughts that brainwash you into believing that you can't have

joy without him, you are guilty of inflicting misery on yourself.) He's already shown you that he doesn't want to be with you in the manner you want to be with him. Calling him and arranging a post breakup hang-out session or two may provide temporary relief from your self-inflicted misery, but it won't provide a permanent remedy for your healing but still aching heart. Calling him will more likely than not start the silly cycle of you and him all over again, ultimately creating even more pain than necessary for you.

With all that said, laughter sounds much more appealing than moping around, willingly inviting misery to keep you company. Stock up on comedies, movies, stand-ups, or anything that will have you throwing your head back, squinting your eyes, and showing off those pearly whites in laughter. Invite close friends and family members over to share in the experience of laughter with you. If laughter can help heal bodies battling illness, it can absolutely assist in healing your aching heart. So make it a point to laugh hard and to laugh often; laugh right through your pain. You may have to force yourself to do this at first. The sadness is intense during immediate post-breakup periods, but the more you laugh, the more you'll want to laugh.

Consider hosting a comedy marathon a couple weekends out of the month. Invite Rickey Smiley, Mike Epps, Chris Tucker, Kevin Hart, Chris Rock, Jamie Foxx, and all of The Kings (or Tha Kangs) of Comedy over. Serve barbeque wings, chips and dip, and margaritas (sugar, no salt, please). Get comfy. And laugh until tears roll down your face and your abs pain you. You'll soon be laughing over cocktails with your besties—at your ex-boo's expense.

What are some of the benefits of laughter?

1. It's *so* much fun to laugh. Denying yourself fun is like denying yourself a giant bowl of ice cream with gummy bears on top—it just doesn't make sense.

2. Laughter helps to preserve your youth and good looks. It blocks stress. And we all know that too much stress will have a twenty-five-year-old looking as if she's fifty-five. Stress grays your hair and expands your waistline. (No thank you! I'll pass on that.)

3. Laughter looks so good on you. People who enjoy laughing are inviting. Don't you love being

around people who can make you laugh or people who enjoy laughing?

4. Laughter is like a mini-workout. We burn calories when we laugh. In addition, laughter tightens those abs. It's your choice: tighter abs or belly jelly? (I'll take an order of tighter abs, please.)

If, for some strange reason, you opt out of the laughter plan and opt in to the I-just-want-to-be-sad-for-the-rest-of-my-days plan or the I-can't-be-happy-without-him plan, ask your-self this question: is *he* moping around, inviting misery to keep *him* company? Answer: Um, let me think about this one for a quick second. I'm going to have to emphatically say, "I doubt it!" I'd put money on him hanging out on the basket-ball court, the golf course, the baseball diamond, the bowling lanes, the pool hall, the skating rink, Mike's man cave—or just about anywhere that denies misery a VIP pass—before I put money on him sitting at home, keeping company with misery's nasty-attitude-having, miserable self.

4

S^3 = Sassy, Spicy, and Single

You have brains in your head. You have

feet in your shoes. You can steer yourself

in any direction you choose. You're on

your own. And you know what

you know. You are the [gal]

who'll decide where to go.

♥ Dr. Seuss

You're accepting the breakup as a lesson learned, an opportunity for personal growth, a blessing in disguise. You're momentarily living life in the Single Lane. But that's *no* excuse to be bland. It's *only* an excuse to regain or even better…upgrade your sassy and your spicy.

Sassy: *Lively, bold, and full of spirit.*
Spicy: *Exciting! Flavorful!*

Being single and miserable, or miserably single, should not be your adopted style of choice…not ever! Singlehood is a time to make your life as flavorful as humanely possible. Have fun—and loads of it. Fun can and must be had in a variety of ways. Hanging out with your family, having slumber parties with your besties, salsa dancing, and wine and painting parties are just a few examples of how to keep fun and flavorful times in your life. Who said you had to be a certified event planner to act as one? Keep your calendar filled with awesome activities and exciting events, like jewelry parties, facials and fondue parties, polish parties, cocktail parties, skating parties, toy parties (wink, wink), and more.

Consider hosting movie nights, game nights, and taco and guacamole nights. You and your besties can rotate planning and hosting events. Events can be potluck styled so your pockets are not worn thin in the name of having a good time. Send out cutesy Evites for your sassy, spicy, and single slumber parties, spa dates, or mani-pedi dates. Bring an amazing attitude and a bright smile to each and every event. Keep your camera phone close by so you can capture your sassy and spicy moments. And last but certainly not least, make certain, at every single event, to have loads of fun and loads of laughs and loads of spice and loads of sass!

In addition to being a girl who just wants to have fun, chase new experiences and opportunities so you can gain new perspectives on yourself and the world around you. Travel. Visit places— near and far—you've always wanted to venture to. Take thousands (not literally) of pictures while you're visiting so you can reminisce about and relive your wonderful experiences over and over again. What else have you always wanted to do but failed to find the time, energy, or courage to? Start a polish line? Attend a painting class? Zumba dancing? Pole dancing (the classes for fun and exercise, not the ones for profit)? Skydiving? Snorkeling? Write a book? Start a business? Enroll in cosmetology school or nursing school? You're operating in "Me Zone" now. Me Zone affords you the luxury and the pleasure of being and doing you. This is the perfect time to embark on a deliberate pursuit of what you want. Just go for it…whatever "it" may be.

While creating fun and chasing new experiences, let us not neglect the art of staying fresh-to-death ("fresh-to-death" as defined by the Urban Dictionary is a term used to describe something that is so good it is unexplainable; well dressed, fashionable, cool until the very end). You're a beautiful woman. And your outer beauty should be in sync with your inner beauty. Hot hair, complementary fashions, well-selected jewelry pieces, picture-perfect polish, a sparkling smile, glowing skin, confidence, a healthy body, and a pleasant attitude are all needed accessories in keeping your overall beauty—inner and outer—synchronized.

Sassy and Spicy Accessories

1. **Hot Hair:** Hot, healthy, clean, well-styled hair is an absolute must! Hot hair sets the tone for your grand entrance. Whether you prefer it long or short, curly or straight, jet-black or bright red, relaxed or natural…just keep it hot!

2. **Healthy Skin:** Using the right cleansers and moisturizers, getting adequate rest, taking your vitamins, eating plenty of fruits and vegetables, and drinking lots of water will help to give your skin a healthy, radiant, sun-kissed glow.

3. **Mascara:** This is an absolute beauty must-have! Mascara makes your eyes come alive.

It gives them pop! I love, love, love Maybelline's Blackest Black Great Lash Mascara (it comes in the classic pink tube and it makes my eyelashes look so rich and dark). I'm sure you have your favorites as well. Just remember to never leave the house without black (or navy) cream coating those lashes.

4. **Lip Gloss:** This is another absolute must-have! MAC has so many beautiful, rich colors. I'm a personal fan of *Pop Mode* and *Desire*. Sephora also has beautiful, long-lasting colors that give your lips a nice tinted shine. My Sephora favorite happens to be *Sangria* with its reddish-bronze tint and glitter accents (Spicy!). It really doesn't matter if you're a MAC girl, a Sephora girl, or a Cover Girl, the most important thing is that

you're a fan of lip shine. Dry, chapped, pale lips versus moisturized, colorful, glistening lips? Um, sign me up for the gloss, please.

5. **Manicured and Pedicured Nails:** You deserve to treat yourself to weekly professional or DIY manicures and pedicures. Soft hands and feet, displaying perfectly filed nails, tamed cuticles, and vibrant colors, are attractive and ladylike. Manicured nails send a subtle message—I subscribe to taking care of and pampering myself, because I'm worth it.

6. **Jewelry:** Jewelry is a girl's bestie! A beautiful pair of earrings, some arm candy—watches and bracelets—or a lovely necklace really helps to complete your look. Rocking your

signature pieces is yet another opportunity to display your signature style.

7. **Perfume:** Perfume is a girl's other bestie! I love Bright Crystal by Versace, Vera Wang by Vera Wang, and Jennifer Aniston by Jennifer Aniston. They all smell so feminine, so lovely, so delicate, so refreshing. Determine which scent(s) you love best, and make it/them your signature.

8. **Put-Together Outfits:** This doesn't mean you have to go into debt trying to own a purple-label wardrobe or that you have to spend half your hard-earned money on red bottoms or that you have to make grocery store runs in evening gowns. I heard a long time ago it's not *what* you wear but *how* you wear it. Clean,

coordinated, appropriate, and affordable with your own special style twist is perfect. Walking around presenting yourself to the world looking like a Sloppy Jane, however, is inexcusable.

9. **A Healthy Body:** Keeping up with a fitness regimen—gym visits, running, walking, Zumba classes, toning exercises, yoga, cardio workouts, weight lifting—is important. Maintaining a healthy body weight, moving your body so your heart can get pumping, keeping your blood pressure down, getting enough sleep, and eating the right foods are key health components. Taking care of yourself, inside and out, enables you to present your best, fierce, and fabulous self to the world on a daily basis. This doesn't mean we all have to be a size two. But determine what your healthy best is and rock it!

10. **A Healthy Va-Jay-Jay:** Making those annual and/or biannual trips to the gynecologist is a non-negotiable for our feminine health. Your gynecologist has the tools and resources needed to get up in there and ensure that everything is on the up-and-up. Remember to always engage in smart and safe sex, *if* you're engaging at all. Make sure he's sporting a pro-phylactic (condom, raincoat, scuba gear, glove, jimmy, body armor, hard hat, strap, Ziploc) each and every time. He's to put one on prior to *any* areas located immediately below the belly button touching! If he opts not to use protec-tion…then, without hesitation or reservation, opt *not* to sleep with him. Your first priority is keeping your body healthy (and pregnant free until baby planning season)….NOT his pleas-ure. If you meet a gentleman who meets your

standards and you believe that you two are in an exclusive, committed relationship, each of you should be tested for all STDs and STIs prior to engaging in sex without the use of protection. **Note**: *Abstaining until marriage is the safest and best sex option.*

11. **Confidence:** Walk tall with your head held high, your shoulders back, and your chest out (but not all the way out). Stride boldly and in confidence. You were fearfully and wonderfully made (that came straight from the Bible). Believe it. Think it. Breathe it. Act like it. Be in tune with what's wonderfully amazing about you—your warm personality, your kindness, your smarts, your problem-solving skills, your ambition, your loyalty, your smile, your caring nature, and more. You're

worthy of daily celebration. Positively affirm and celebrate yourself every day. Keep your thoughts on Channel Positive. Repetitive, positive thinking attracts positivity into your life. #KeepItPositive

Positive Affirmations

- ♥ I am special.
- ♥ I am worthy.
- ♥ Love loves me.
- ♥ I am a beautiful woman.
- ♥ I bless everything I touch.
- ♥ My possibilities are endless!
- ♥ I have a lot to offer the world.
- ♥ I am deserving of amazing love.
- ♥ My life has meaning and purpose.
- ♥ Abundant peace and abundant joy belong to me.

♥ I have all the smarts, resources, and support needed to meet my dreams.

♥ God loves me! He thinks I'm something like a big deal. That makes me something like a big deal!

12. **A Positive Attitude:** Be pleasant. Put the cussing, fussing, and complaining on ice. No "funktitudes" are allowed. Let someone else rock the catty, funky, stank, petty, combative, nasty, argumentative, negative "fml" attitude. Opt to have a pleasant and positive disposition. Opt to smile at others and to display manners. Opt to show kindness and class. Opt to be genuine and caring. Opt to see the glass as half full. Opt to make lemonade out of the occasional lemons of life. Opt to treat people with respect and dignity. Opt to

treat yourself with respect and dignity. Opt to entertain laughter and fun times. And opt always to be grateful for your blessings. Of course, this doesn't mean you'll never have today-is-not-the-day and I-am-not-the-one days, but this attitude should never, ever be adopted as your primary attitude or disposition of choice. Opt OUT on funk and negativity. Opt IN on joy and positivity. (Emphasis on opt because we choose our attitudes.) #StayRockinAPositveAttitude

When equipped with all your sassy, spicy, and single accessories, you'll walk into a room, and all eyes will focus on you. Notice will be taken of your attention to health and style, your grace, your quiet confidence, your positive vibes, and how well put together and kept together you are.

People will see a beautiful, confident, self-loving, self-respecting, fearless, and single woman who is living in and enjoying her moment. They will want a sample of what you have to offer, because you make being single look crazy-hot! Having fun, trying new things, dream chasing, and living life on your own terms, all while keeping it fresh-to-death? Now that's a recipe for Sassy, Spicy, and Single living!

5

101 "I Just Can't" Deal Breakers!

No one can drive us crazy

unless we give them the keys.

♥ ***Doug Houston***

*I*t takes a lot of work finding your way back to you after a hurtful and painful breakup. You don't want any of your hard work to become undone. We just *can't* allow that to happen. With all that said, here is a list of 101 unhealthy philosophies and behaviors that just can't be accepted, adopted, and/or practiced on our continuing journeys and in our new relationships.

Read and reference each of the following deal breakers as often as needed on your journeys:

1. I just *can't* be lazy about finding and seeing the beauty, the worth, and the value in me. For if others are charged with finding and seeing the beauty, worth, and value in me, there's a possibility that my beauty, worth, and value will *not* be accurately assessed.

2. I just *can't* depend on a guy to determine how worthy, how meaningful, how special, how lovable, or how valuable I am. It's my duty to make these determinations first.

3. I just *can't* put myself last.

4. I just *can't* play the role of Good-Enough Girl! I have way too much to offer.

5. I just *can't* be cowardly in making decisions regarding my well-being.

6. I just *can't* forget to love myself more.

7. I just *can't* chase, beg, negotiate, or belittle myself for a man's love and/or commitment.

8. I just *can't* chase, beg, negotiate, or belittle myself for the attention of a man.

9. I just *can't* operate as if I possess NO power or have NO authority over my life.

10. I just *can't* forget that I'm obligated to teach people how to treat me. I can't slip on *my* obligation and allow others to teach me how I'm to be treated.

11. I just *can't* think negatively about myself. I am to be my own number-one fan and biggest cheerleader always.

12. I just *can't* play the role of Secret Lover. I deserve more than being kept a behind-closed-doors secret.

13. I just *can't* be an attention junkie, willing to do anything and everything for *any* type of attention.

14. I just *can't* tolerate being bullied in my relationships.

15. I just *can't* wait *indefinitely* for a guy to determine MY future.

16. I just *can't* accept and justify a guy's suspicious behavior simply because I want to keep him around.

17. I just *can't* accept and make excuses for shortcomings in my relationship.

18. I just *can't* enable my relationship to hold me back or hold me down.

19. I just *can't* adopt an I'm-not-good-enough mentality. I'm MORE than good enough for true love, respect, peace, and joy.

20. I just *can't* accept and believe that real love has to hurt.

21. I just *can't* cosign...on anything (apart-ments, cars, loans, etc.) for a guy I'm not married to.

22 *a*. I just *can't* abandon the safest sex option— abstinence until marriage.

22 *b*. If I do decide to engage in sexual activities before marriage, I just *can't* be charmed out of practicing safe sex...ever.

23. I just *can't* be pressured into sleeping with a guy until I am 100% confident that I am really ready to.

24. I just *can't* entertain men who are married. I refuse to be a married man's girlfriend in holding.

25. I just *can't* give a guy a pass to treat me as if I'm a doormat!

26. I just *can't* accept that I'm not worthy, lovable, or special enough to meet an amazing man (in due season).

27. I just *can't* agree to be a Side Girl (or a Girl On The Side)! I deserve a mate's full commitment and undivided attention.

28. I just *can't* fail to remember that I always have options.

29. I just *can't* be so terrified of being alone that I'm willing to put up with negativity in a relationship.

30. I just *can't* settle for any random guy in my impatience in waiting for an amazing man. An amazing man is worth waiting for.

31. I just *can't* play the role of the Thirsty Chick! **Role Description**: *A woman who oozes desperation, craves any kind of attention, and is willing to sell her soul for that attention.*

32. I just *can't* anticipate not being treated with dignity and respect in a relationship, because I don't love myself enough to *believe* I deserve to be treated any better.

33. I just *can't* abandon my smarts in making decisions regarding my relationships and my well-being.

34. I just *can't* forget that single does **NOT** mean desperate!

35. I just *can't* set low standards and have minimum expectations for myself and how I'm to be treated in a relationship. I am to anticipate and expect being treated well, not poorly.

36. I just *can't* be afraid to say good-bye if I'm not being treated well in my relationship.

37. I just *can't* think and speak negatively about what true love has to offer me.

38. I just *can't* accept that chivalry no longer exists.

39. I just *can't* put myself last. I must always take care of me.

40. I just *can't* ignore my gut, my intuition, or relationship red flags, because I'm too afraid to deal with the root of an issue.

41. I just *can't* continuously give more than I receive.

42. I just *can't* live in suffering and misery for the sake of keeping up with The Relation-ship Joneses.

43. I just *can't* allow for my body to be abused in any way! I am not to abuse my own body in any way! Others will have no choice but to follow my lead.

44. I just *can't* act as if I'm OK with mess I'm not *really* OK with.

45. I just *can't* accept being spoken to in a manner that is degrading or disrespectful.

46. I just *can't* tolerate being debased.

47. I just *can't* enable others to control or manipulate me.

48. I just *can't* be told that my feelings don't matter.

49. I just *can't* be treated as if my feelings don't matter.

50. I just can't adopt an I'm-not-beautiful men-tality. I'm a beautiful woman who has a lot to offer the world!

51. I just *can't* be silenced when I have some-thing important to say.

52. I just *can't* accept being trapped in an unfulfilling relationship. I can always use my wings to fly on and fly free if need be.

53. I just *can't* confuse sex with love. I just can't believe that a man loves me simply because he's willing to have sex with me.

54. I just *can't* believe that attaching myself to a mate is the remedy for a lack of self-love. I must put in the work needed to truly love and feel good about being me first.

55. I just *can't* be content with mediocrity in a relationship. I deserve and should expect more than just OK in my relationships.

56. I just *can't* sacrifice my emotional well-being for a relationship.

57. I just *can't* forget to find a reason to fall in love with myself…everyday.

58. I just *can't* accept infidelity as the norm in my relationships.

59. I just *can't* stay in a relationship and endure foolishness, suffering, and heartache simply because I'm too afraid to be alone.

60. I just *can't* accept that there are no more good men walking around in the world!

61. I just *can't* accept the role of Bitter Chick! **Role Description***: A woman who is mad at the world; possessing a nasty attitude; holding on to past disappointments; unwilling to forgive and invite joy back in.* I can learn to forgive and let anger and

resentment go. In addition, I can still have joy like a river overflowing. I just have to claim it.

62. I just *can't* accept words as truth, for words alone can be dressed up and misleading. His words must be accompanied by actions that back up his promises.

63. I just *can't* view inconsistency as a relationship norm.

64. I just *can't* accept being only tolerated in my relationships; I deserve to feel wanted, adored, and celebrated!

65. I just *can't* accept that a relationship has the right to stress me out.

66. I just *can't* forget or neglect to put my faith, confidence, and trust in God.

67. I just *can't* lose myself in my mate.

68. I just *can't* believe and accept that I'm ONLY deserving of poor treatment in a relationship. I am not to accept that poor treatment is all I'm good enough for.

69. I just *can't* entertain a man who is not worthy of my trust.

70. I just *can't* let myself go! I am to take the time and care required to be and to present my best self on a daily basis.

71. I just *can't* go Dutch on first dates!

72. I just *can't* neglect my morals or my values for the sake of being in a relationship.

73. I just *can't* be with a lazy man who doesn't see the value in hard work.

74. I just *can't* be with a man who isn't concerned with protecting and providing for me.

75. I just *can't* fail to remember that the privilege of a lifetime is to be exactly who I am.

76. I just *can't* forget that I'll become exactly what I believe myself to be.

77. I just *can't* put myself down.

78. I just *can't* forget, no matter the situation, to always remain in a state of gratitude. I'm to be grateful for every blessing extended my way.

79. I just *can't* be with a man whom I feel I have to spy on or babysit!

80. I just *can't* compare my journey to the journeys of others. My journey has been uniquely designed just for me.

81. I just *can't* forget that I'm a masterpiece in God's eyes.

82. I just *can't* forget to treat myself well.

83. I just *can't* leave God out of my relationships.

84. I just *can't* play the role of the Jump-Off! **Role Description:** *You'll never be taken out in public on dinner or movie dates; you'll only be taken to his bedroom. You'll never be engaged in meaningful or stimulating conversation; you'll only be engaged in sex talk. You'll never be highly regarded or respected; you'll just be regarded as the girl who fulfills his sexual pleasures. You'll never meet his mom, dad, sister, or close friends; you'll only meet his sheets.*

85. I just *can't* find skinny jeans on a man attractive!

86. I just *can't* find pants hanging off of boxer-covered hind parts sexy! That's the epitome of disgusting!

87. I just *can't* waste my time on guys who don't have the capacity required to go the

distance with me. My time is much too precious and valuable.

88. I just *can't* be told that I don't have the right to ask a potential mate about his past relationships.

89. I just *can't* view my past boyfriends as wastes of time. They were all teachers who taught me valuable lessons.

90. I just *can't* neglect my friends and my family because I'm in a relationship.

91. I just *can't* speak negatively to or about myself. I am to give myself positive praise daily.

92. I just *can't* position myself as simply a guy's Entertainment Girl! I am more than a cheap, temporary thrill.

93. I just *can't* allow a guy to treat me as if I'm a nonfactor! I'm to always remember that I'm a factor, I'm important, and I matter!

94. I just *can't* waste my time entertaining guys who are total non-contenders.

95 *a*. I just *can't* forget to love myself.

95 *b*. I just *can't* forget that God loves me.

96. I just *can't* forget to pray for guidance and direction in my life and on my journey.

97. I just *can't* accept that it's OK to be in a relationship that makes me cry my life away.

98. I just *can't* forget to create my own joy and make my *own* fun! I can't depend on others to do it for me.

99. I just *can't* forget to embrace my strength.

100. I just *can't* fall apart and crumble over a failed relationship.

101. I just *can't* forget that I'm a very special lady who deserves to be treated in a very special way.

Girl, Don't You Dare!

You better not dare!

♥ *Unknown*

*L*adies: In extension and in some cases elaboration of our list of "Just *Can't*" Deal Breakers, here are some behaviors and philosophies that we won't *dare* accept, adopt, and/or practice on our continuing journeys.

1. Don't you dare subscribe to being a Bitter Babe! It's unattractive, unflattering, and

unsexy. It takes way more effort and energy to hate people than it does to forgive them and move on. Release yourself, and the person or persons you feel have hurt you in the past, from emotional captivity. Release the anger and disappointment over the relationship failing to be all you hoped it would be. It will feel as if weights are being lifted off your shoulders. This will allow you to journey happier, more peacefully, and without the heaviness of anger weighing you down.

P.S. Give yourself an open invitation to get back to the sweets of life.

2. Don't you dare subscribe to being a Low-Self-Esteem-Having Honey! Invest the time and work needed to love and feel good about

being you. Invest the time and work needed to hold yourself in such high regard that you don't tolerate nonsense, making sure that you're not hanging onto just about anybody simply for the sake of being with *somebody*. It's NOT always better to have a man than to have no man at all, especially a man who mistreats you or a man who refuses to, for whatever reason or reasons, give you what you want and what you need out of a relationship. Men who are granted the privilege of sharing time and space with you should be of a certain caliber. You, along with your time, are extremely valuable and extremely precious. Think it. Know it. Believe it. Act like it.

3. Don't you dare be afraid of being alone! Embrace being alone as an opportunity to

learn how to become an even *better* you. In addition, use the time to reconnect and rebuild an even deeper connection with God. At times, our relationship with God (as well as with ourselves) takes a backseat when we become overly preoccupied with and indulged in our mates. Being alone can afford you the time and space needed to reboot your relationship with God and with yourself. Rushing into new relationships or holding onto unhealthy ones will not allow you the time needed to restore yourself.

4. Don't you dare operate as a Thirsty Chick! When you're desperately searching for *any* and *every* guy to give you a little attention and being heavily dependent on him (or them) to make you feel relevant, men will detect this

instantly. You look thirsty! Your transparent desperation then becomes your weakness. You're the prey, and he'll be the predator who cleverly sets the trap so he can pounce. What's the trap? *Game*. What's game? Him telling you exactly what he knows you want to hear so he can get exactly what he wants while applying the *least* amount of energy, effort, work, commitment, and dedication possible. And because you're so "thirsty," you're *temporarily* content (but not thoroughly quenched) with his far from impressive "presentation" of interest in you.

5. Don't you dare associate your relevance with whom you're dealing with or whom you're *not* dealing with! Being you and you alone has already secured you a seat on the

Relevancy Bus. You're already valid. You're *already* someone special simply because you are who you are. You don't need a cosigner on that so you're free to stop looking for one.

6. Don't you dare suffer in vain! Use the lessons you've learned from past relationships to assist you in making smarter relationship choices and setting higher demands in future relationships.

7. Don't you dare settle for less than you are worth! Evaluate your relationship credentials and what you bring to the relationship. Be clear on exactly what you want and need from a relationship based on your credentials and what you are willing to offer. If a potential mate can't match your deposit, then *former* potential mate can keep it moving.

8. Don't you dare compromise who you are and what you *really* want! Recognize your worth, govern yourself accordingly, and require others to treat you in a manner that is in alignment with your worth.

9. Don't you dare forget to trust God! He sits high, but He looks low. He'll never forsake you. God knows what's best for us far better than we do and He'll never position us where He can't cover us.

10. Don't you dare forget to live in the moment! You don't have to sit around waiting for Mr. Good Man to make himself known before giving yourself permission to love life and take advantage of all life has to offer you. Live in the right now. Laugh hard. Play hard. Travel.

Make fond memories with friends and family. Find a hobby. Be creative. Seek healthy adventures. Mr. Good Man will present himself in due season. In the interim, keep doing you and be deliberate about enjoying your precious gift—your life.

11. Don't you dare forget to be daring! Create a list of all the fun, creative, and exciting things you'd absolutely love to do and dare to tackle that list. Create a list of all the goals you'd like to accomplish. Work diligently on introducing those dreams to your reality. Dare to be adventurous! Dare to be courageous! Dare to be bold!

12. Don't you dare forget to rock a spirit of gratitude! Thank God for the rain that promotes

growth. Thank God for the sunshine that *always* appears after the rain.

13. Don't you dare forget to love and appreciate yourself! You are special and amazing! That's worth daily appreciation and daily celebrations!

14. Don't you dare forget how powerful you truly are! You have the power to call the shots in *your* life. Always remember, no matter the situation, that you are a powerful and skillful shot caller.

15. Don't you dare be afraid to say Boy Bye! if your mate is not treating you in accordance with how you deserve and desire to be treated.

16. Don't you dare be afraid to love again and to put yourself back out there when you meet

an amazing man who is willing to put in *all* the work required to prove he's more than just another guy.

17. Don't you dare sabotage future relationships that have the potential to be special, meaningful, and long-lasting. This can be particularly difficult not to do after being hurt and disappointed by love in the past. Your guards are way up, your defense mechanisms are in overdrive, and your willingness to trust again, in the name of love, is on reluctan*t*. However, you have to work extremely hard at not allowing the behavior of Johnny Came Real Wrong to negatively impact what Coming Correct Kevin is trying to build with you.

Note: *You don't have to be terribly afraid of participating in the game of love once again because you've drawn up new plays for your Playbook of Love. These plays outline your elevated standards and expectations; what you'll tolerate and what are total deal breakers. In addition, your new playbook has you positioned as a player of power as opposed to a player with no power or authority. You know how to handle yourself if Relationship Foolishness presents its foolish head. As a result, you should have no worries and complete confidence in yourself and in your ability to make healthier relationship decisions.*

7

Rock Your Moment!

We delight in the beauty of the butterfly, but rarely admit the changes it has gone through to achieve that beauty.

♥ **Maya Angelou**

*C*ongratulations! Thanks to your dedication and hard work you are more than well on your way. You're a beautiful woman who has been through some stuff. You've taken some emotional licks and endured a series of unwanted heartaches. You were almost declared an emotional homicide, but you cried, fought, prayed, laughed, and willed your way back to life. You've taken the time needed to delicately and piece-by-piece put yourself back together. Your strength and your courage are quite admirable and sexy.

As a result of your strength and courage, you're now 100% foolish-man free. You're drama-free, stress-free, and consumed-days-of-sadness-free. You're agony-free, trying-to-figure-out-what-in-the-world-happened-free, believing-that-you're-inadequate-free, pleading-and-begging-free, sleepless-nights-free, settling-for-less-free, confusion-free, doubt-free, and tear-free. Free at last! Free at last! Thanking God ALMIGHTY to be free at last!

You're finally believing and buying into the notion that you are OK, that you're going to continue being OK. This realization is accompanied by an upgraded confidence in yourself. You're learning that you're stronger than you ever thought you were. You're setting new and elevated standards for how people will treat you. You're refocusing and re-prioritizing. You're back at the top of your priority list—where you should've always been. You're prayed-up and determined to stay that way. You're releasing feelings of anger and resentment in order to make space for even more peace and joy. Bag lady? Not you! You've unloaded all the emotional baggage you have accrued from past hurts, and you left those old bags at the curb. You've graciously tipped the baggage handler, told him to discard the unwanted and unneeded bags in the nearest Dumpster, and now you're traveling on your merry, light way…ready to continue enjoying your journey.

You're feeling good and taking much better care of yourself now—emotionally, physically, and spiritually. You're smiling a little brighter, laughing a little louder, and looking a lot more fabulous (eliminating stress and sleepless nights from your life has an anti-aging effect). You're not putting your happiness on hold while waiting for something to happen. You're declaring that you'll be happy right where you are planted. You're not waiting for happiness to kindly pay you a visit and whisk you away to a place named Bliss; instead, you're making happy happen. You're learning that you don't have to desperately depend on anyone or any particular situation for your joy and happiness, because joy and happiness are already within you.

Your self-esteem is back on full. You're no longer seeking validation from outside sources because you've determined and declared that you're the ultimate Boss Chick; you're the most "beautifulest" girl in the world, and a price can't be placed on how special and valuable you are. You're no longer seeking someone to cosign on your certificate of validation. You know that you're somebody special because YOU said so and because you're making it so. And even more importantly because God designed it so.

You're not thirsty for the approval or attention of each and every man, because loving and appreciating yourself first is quenching your thirst. Your charming personality is breaking through more easily because you've done (and you're continuing to do) your due diligence in purging from your system all that doesn't promote growth: anger, resentment, holding grudges, bitterness, and behaving like a victim. You've turned challenges, setbacks, and disappointments into lessons, opportunities, and wins. You're looking even better in your present and in your future than you ever looked in your past. You took Beyoncé's lead and found the good in good-bye.

You now know that you're more powerful than you ever could've imagined being. You recovered that same power you once allowed past mates full possession of. You're exercising control over your choices, your steps, and your moves; you are no longer willing to operate from a state of powerlessness. You've stepped out on your fears and met up with your courage. And now that you've snatched your power back and upgraded your confidence, people better move out of your way! You're a sassy, spicy single who's on the move. You've broken free from the covering of dependency and powerlessness feeling refreshed, rejuvenated, encouraged, and empowered. Your wings are full-grown, and you're getting your fly on. You're ready to take it to the next level and get your soar on.

You should be very proud of yourself! It takes a great deal of strength, courage, discipline, faith, and sass to battle back from heartbreak. Your commitment and dedication to recovering from, as opposed to surrendering to, heartbreak is worthy of applause. Wear your sassy, spicy, unwilling-to-settle, single badge with pride. Take a minute to reflect on how far you've come in the process of journeying back to you. Appreciate your season and all the wonderfulness it has to offer you. Embrace the healthier, happier, more independent, stronger, more confident, empowered, and bolder you.

You're a beautiful woman who has found her way back...

The End

8

Boy Bye! Extras

*T*he following entries are *Boy Bye!* extras that blend events and scenarios with my thoughts and observations on women and relationships.

No Work...No Prize!

Will a boxer ever be decorated with the championship belt *prior* to taking some hard hits to the dome, delivering some one-two punch combinations to his opponent, and devoting his blood, sweat, and tears into being declared the victor? Will a track star ever be graced with the shiny golden medal *prior* to taking off like lightning at the sound of the signaling gunshot, enduring the distance, and outlasting his competition? Would the Miami Heat have ever been rewarded with platinum and diamond 2012 championship rings, crisp white championship tees, and fitted championship hats *prior* to consistently executing effective plays, creating shots, knocking down buckets after buckets, hustling back on defense, eliminating team after team, battling the Celtics' Big Three (And what a battle it was! The Celtics did not go down without a fight!), and outplaying the eager and talented players of Oklahoma City? Absolutely not! Rewards come *after* we've proven ourselves worthy; *after* we've demonstrated that we have what it takes to be a champion.

You are a prize! Worthy of only being secured, obtained, claimed, or touched by a champion. You're like the shiny, larger-than-life trophy all the NBA players dream of touching and raising up at the end of the season. You are like the shiny gold medal all the Olympians work their tails off to have draped around their necks on the raised podium. You are like the golden, decorative belt boxing champs envision having fastened around their waist after hard training and hard hitting. If he's trying to be with you—Ms. Prize—he'll have to prove he's a champion. How can he *prove* he's a champion? He proves he's a champion by being a man of his word; by operating with integrity; by treating you like a lady—like a prize—always; by respecting you, your body, and your wishes consistently; by being kind, generous, and considerate with you; by making you, your feelings, and your well-being a priority; by showing you that he appreciates you; by being present when you need him; by being another source of peace and calm in your life as opposed to a source of stress and chaos; by being patient, loving, and understanding with you; by convincing you that he's a hero.

Giving out prizes, gold medals, and championship rings prematurely is silly and unheard of. Similarly, handing out relationship "prizes"— unconditional love, care, support, intimacy, and more prematurely is silly (but unfortunately not unheard of). If he's unwilling to put in all the hard work and dedication required to secure the prize of you then it's probably a great idea to have him "keep it movin." You're not checking for just another regular guy anyway. You're checking for a champion. You're checking for a hero. #ChampCheck

Taking My Talents Elsewhere

s we all know, or *should* know by now, Ray Allen has taken his skills and talents south. He's bringing some additional heat to Miami! Upon hearing the news of his decision to venture south, I was shocked, confused, and a little…just a little…okay, *a lot* brokenhearted. My beloved Celtics were supposed to always stay intact—in my mind, anyway. According to speculations, Allen was disheartened with how he had been treated during the end of his final season with the C's—trade talks and losing his starting spot to the young and up-and-coming Avery Bradley. In addition, it was rumored that he and Rondo had a deteriorating relationship. And although I'll always love the original Big Three/Four, and I never, ever wanted to see the group busted up, I can't be mad (unlike KG) with Ray Allen for making his move.

It's not uncommon to find yourself at a personal crossroads in a relationship. You may find yourself feeling underappreciated and borderline disposable. You have a decision to make. Am I going to the left or am I going to the right, you ask yourself. Do you stay, deal with it, and stick it out in the name of loyalty? Do you factor in the length of time invested? And if so, how much time does one have to unhappily invest before he/she can not only be set free but set free...free of guilt? Do you abandon your own desires and put your energy into trying to make or force it—the relationship—to work, hoping with your everything that things will somehow get better?

Or...do you clean out your locker, turn in your team jersey, and ultimately declare that you've given the relationship all that you had to give, stating that you're deeply disappointed in your investment return, that you served your time and honored your commitment to the best of your ability, and that you're now more concerned with your own personal happiness and peace of mind than in making the relationship work? Do you announce that you are now taking your skills and talents elsewhere? So many questions, but only you'll have the answers if you ever find yourself in a similar predicament.

When making your crossroads decision, honesty (being honest with yourself) must be the greatest factor. If you *honestly* see the potential and believe in the likelihood of your relationship moving in a healthy direction, then you give it an honest chance. If you're *honestly* miserable, *honestly* see no value in hanging around, *honestly* feel the relationship does not have the capacity to move in a healthy direction…then you may want to strongly consider "moving to the left."

Wishing you all the best with your new squad #34 (the former #20 of Team Black and Green).

Are You Valid...Yet?

~~~

You're beautiful—so beautiful that foundation, gloss, shadow, and mascara are honored and delighted to acquaint themselves with your face. You've managed to delay the signs of aging by keeping yourself fit and healthy. You're graceful, loving, caring, unique, sassy, giving, intelligent, and more. Your family adores you and swears you're the hottest ticket in town. They brag about you tirelessly to friends, coworkers, neighbors, people down at the church, and to just about anyone else who meets the sad misfortune of being forced to listen to your cheerleaders rant and rave about your greatness. Your friends admire you— your strength, your easy-going nature, your fashion savvy, your loving spirit, your dedication, and your ability to make things happen. Your coworkers secretly envy your professional charisma, how gutsy you are, and your go-getter mentality.

You're "something like a big deal," a "hot girl," a "five-star" in the eyes and minds of just about everyone around you. There's just one problem. *You* don't view yourself through the same lenses. You don't give yourself nearly enough credit. You fail to see the beauty that is all you. And why is that? Is it because some made-up societal standard has yet to provide an unneeded signature (or cosign unnecessarily) on your validation sticker?

Society's Made Up Standards of Success:

1. Long, flowing hair.

2. A size two.

3. Married by the age of twenty-five.

4. Mother of two by age thirty.

5. Owner of a luxury vehicle.

You view these *unnecessary* co-signings as confirmation that you're actually worthy, actually valuable. And as a result, *you've* counted yourself out; you've deemed yourself invalid, unworthy, and less than.

You've fallen prey to false thoughts and false thinking. Your acceptance of those false thoughts have you believing you're less than amazing, because you're not super teeny or because your skin has more chocolate than vanilla in it or because you're not pushing a Benz. Your acceptance of those false thoughts has you believing that you're worthless because you're not "wifeyed up", "kiddied up", or "whatevered up." You're refusing to believe that you can be your best you, your most beautiful you, unless some man or some possession or some physical attribute is associated with you.

"Chile please" (accompanied by teeth sucking and eyeball rolling)! Miss Lady…your mere existence is more than validation, more than confirmation, that you are "that girl," and that you are more than enough. You are an amazing woman whether you're a size two or a size twenty-two, whether you're riding around town in a shiny silver Benz or on a 54-seater city bus, whether you're banking six figures or barely five, whether you're married or with a new boo or strutting in the single lane, whether you're on mommy duty or you're kiddie-free. This can't be said enough…you are amazing, more than enough, relevant, and valuable! You were *born* that way. Breathe it. Believe it. Act like it. Embrace being you…beyond-validated you. #BeyondValidated

Why Are You Single?

"So...why are you single?" How does one answer *that* question? With a shoulder shrug? By squinting your eyes and repositioning your eyebrows in a let-me-think-about–that-for-a-second gesture? Maybe a blank stare? Or do you simply respond, "I don't know; I just am"? It's an awkward question. It may even be fair to say it's a question that may make some feel a little uncomfortable if it's accompanied by judgment (or perceived judgment).

Question: Why are you single?

Judgmental Thought: If she can't get and keep a man, something *must* be wrong with her! This chick is probably crazy as hell!

I'm assuming most women don't know exactly *why* they are single; they just know that they are. Dating is a gamble. Your dating experience will either be a big hit or a disappointing miss. Similar to gamblers desperately hoping to walk away from the tables in Vegas with big bucks in their pockets, daters hope they've met that person they'll be sharing their last first kiss with. But if another dating situation bites the dust and hits the road, will you deem yourself unworthy of love, of little value, undesirable, or psycho? Although you hoped to win big, the possibility of losing big is very real. Does that keep you from even contending in the next round? If your fear of losing has crippled you, the answer is…absolutely.

If you're willing to let the chips fall where they may, willing to hope for the best but be prepared for the worst, if you're confident that whatever the outcome you'll still be OK, then you continue to wisely gamble with your heart with confidence that, in due season, you'll win big—a happy, healthy relationship. In the interim, accept that you're single because you're supposed to be single. Enjoy friends and family, getting lost in your own thoughts and your alone time, opportunities for growth, being selfish, and dream chasing, and most of all enjoy being you! What God has for you—marriage, children, wealth, promotion, and more—is for you. It has *your* name on it! Just remember…God works in His time (not ours) and in our best interest. We just have to trust Him and be patient.

So the next time you're asked, "Why are *you* single?" you can keep your response short, simple, and sweet, "For now, I'm single because I'm supposed to be."

Just Flow

*I*t can be extremely challenging and frustrating, at times, to go with the flow—Life's flow. Life says, "Up;" we say, "Down." Life says, "Turn right;" we say, "Nah, I want to go to the left." We are in a constant battle or struggle with Life's wishes for our lives. This voluntary struggle prevents us from seeing the beauty, wearing the smiles, and joyriding with Peace and Happiness while in our current stations. We're unwilling to accept that where we are, *temporarily*, is where we actually need to be. For example, some singles devote a high percentage of their time and energy on dreading and fighting being temporarily unemployed in the Love and Romance Department. That energy could and should be channeled much more positively. Focusing thoughts and energy on self-improvement, fostering solid relationships with friends and family, your talents, and your goals are healthy topics of focus.

Think positively, and petition Life for your desires (just be mindful that sometimes what we want is not what we need). While in waiting, declare to appreciate and enjoy your health, your family, your friends, and your creativity. Going with Life's flow by accepting that where we are is where we actually need to be is similar to riding, without protest, an ocean's cool blue wave. At times we try, relentlessly and in vain, to move in the opposite direction of our assigned waves, leaving our arms feeling tired and heavy, our hearts exhausted and feeling as if they were beating over a thousand beats per minute, our legs feeling weak with the strength of boiled spaghetti noodles, and our lungs feeling distressed from all the huffing and puffing. And amazingly, despite all the physical and emotional protesting, we find ourselves *still* exactly where Life wants and needs us to be.

When it's time to make moves, we will absolutely know it. You don't have to force or rush anything. What's for you is for you and for you only. Your journey has been uniquely and purposefully designed just for you. So there's no need to worry about or fight it. Just flow with it...

"Best Thing I Never Had!"

~~~

As I listen to King Bey's (that would be Beyoncé) song, "Best Thing I Never Had," I can't help but feel a sincere appreciation for the sassy, pick-yourself-up, dust-yourself-off, one-clown-doesn't-stop-the-show, I-love-me-more post-breakup female anthem! How many of us can make claims to owning the same exact sentiments the song's feisty one-and two-liners evoke? I love singing along with Bey when she sings… "I bet it sucks to be you right now." Don't we all, at least temporarily, want life without us to suck for the exes? Just a little bit? Like Marsha Ambrosius, we want their new girls to cheat on them with basketball players. Or like Kerri Hilson, we want our exes to be mad we're cuter than the new girls they're with. But while we are secretly wishing a *sucky* life for those who shall remain nameless, we have to be mindful that our energy must be channeled into making certain life doesn't suck for us post-breakup; that we don't become bitter and unwilling to forgive; that we don't lead ourselves into a post-breakup emotional ditch obsessing about what could have been; that we don't continue carrying our old bags from relationship to relationship; that we don't deny peace and joy an all-access pass into our lives because the former relationship didn't go as planned.

Then there's the line, "I used to want you so bad; I'm so through with that." Haven't we all wanted some fella so badly that we thought life couldn't and wouldn't go on without him? Only to learn that life most certainly goes on—and not only does life go on, but if we allow it to, it

will proceed in a more peaceful and joyful manner than we thought possible. The key is *allowing*
life to do so—keeping what's worth keeping from
our experiences and blowing the rest away with a
breath of kindness.

My favorite line in Bey's sassy tune is "Thank
God I found the good in good-bye." Although
good-byes can be painful, we have to force ourselves to see the good in throwing up voluntary,
and at times involuntary, deuces. The good in
good-bye may include but is not limited to: peace
of mind, personal growth, gained experience,
renewed confidence in yourself, and learning that
you're stronger than you thought you were. It may
also include a decrease in the number of hours
filled with tears, stress, confusion, and overana-
lyzing don't-make-a-bit-of-sense behavior and
increased opportunity to meet a gentleman who

has the capacity to go the distance with you. Wow! The blessings in good-byes are *truly* worth celebration!

As I rock out to Bey's song in the shower or the car or at the gym, I think of past loves from my life. I take a moment to appreciate them for the lessons they brought into my life. Then I take another moment to thank them for giving me the opportunity to see, firsthand, that the good in good-byes really does exist. #TheGoodInGoodBye

Keep What is Worth Keeping, and with a Breath of Kindness, Blow the Rest Away....

~~~~~

"**K**eep what's worth keeping, and with a breath of kindness, blow the rest away." We seldom "blow the rest away," especially with a "breath of kindness." Instead, we—and when I say we, I'm referring to anyone and everyone who has been disappointed by love—opt to hold on to past hurts, pressing the replay button so our stories of hurt can play over and over again in our minds. We allow our past hurts to become our identities, to define us, to cripple us. We proudly wear our past hurts as our badges...of honor. A disappointing situation does not define you, it doesn't make you who you are, nor should it dictate all you are to be.

Every time your thoughts take you back to a past hurt or disappointment, press the stop button before the sad storytelling marathon begins. We don't have to tell our same old stories of hurt and pain that have us cast as powerless victims over and over. We can start telling new stories about ourselves; stories in which we're cast as heroines and victors.

Today's a great day to start telling your *new* story…

No Do-Overs, Only Do-Betters

Ran into somebody that I used to be into,

forcing me to ponder, what exactly was I into

regarding said person that I'm no longer into?

♥ *R. Hall*

Despite how badly we may want to rewind time back to the day right *before* we met Mr. Who Shall Remain Nameless and erase the pain and disappointment away, we can't. What we can do is embrace our moving on as evidence that we're strong, smart, and fierce. We can embrace our moving on as evidence that God keeps us in His care even in our lowest, saddest, and most confusing moments. We can allow our pasts to serve as guides and as manuals. We'll apply the lessons of yesterday to today in making healthier choices for our lives.

Who cares if we don't get any do-overs? At least we can thank God for opportunities to do things a little bit better next time. #CheersToDoBetters

Seven Tips for Dating

You've met a gentleman who, based on initial impressions, may have the potential to become a dating contender. However, before you get in too deep, here are some simple tips you may find useful.

1. Ask for proof of identification. Believe it or not, some people are not opposed to providing false information about their full name, age, and place of residence.

2. Do your research! Look him up in a public records search. Information can be found on his age, employment history, place(s) of residence, criminal history, marital status, and

family background (For example, does he have any children he conveniently forgot to tell you about?). Note: He does NOT have to know that you are trying your detective skills out. You're doing your homework but you don't want him to think you're a stalker.

3. Ask questions! Ask direct questions about his prior relationships. If he's evasive and unwilling to share, that may be a red flag. Ask questions about his dating intentions and don't fall for fluff. Men can be very convincing with their words. They know most women want a commitment. Be aware of the guys who may just be telling you what he knows you want to hear.

4. Be smart! This is an add-on to number three. If he tells you he wants a commitment, but

his actions don't support that statement, then two plus two... not totaling four. Don't be so happy to have a guy around that you abandon your smarts. Rely on your smarts, your experiences, and your intuition. And assess him on his actions...not just his fancy words.

5. Take your time in getting to learn more about him. Don't feel pressured to move at a pace that you are uncomfortable with.

6. Follow your gut. Listen to yourself. Trust yourself. If your inner voice is telling you, "Something is off here," believe it! Don't try to shush it just because you're happy to have a new guy around.

7. If he's shared his ID, has no secret record/ wife/children, is open and honest about past relationships, you don't think that he's trying to fluff you, his actions are consistent with his words, he welcomes you taking your time, and your instincts are not sending you warning signals, then enjoy the moment. Take it one date at a time. Be your genuine self. Be open to new possibilities. Stay smart. And have fun.

Love and Basketball

*B*asketball happens to be my favorite sport of all time. I fell in love with Basketball shortly after being introduced to *him* during my high school years. I was a proud Lady Charger my entire high school career. In my fantasy, I'd liken myself to King James; in reality my skills were (and most likely still are) more like the player who comes into the game when his or her team is up by twenty points with approximately ten seconds left on the game clock. Nonetheless, this sport will always have my heart. And this is probably why I find myself comparing love and relationships to my beloved Basketball. In the game of love (and yes, love is absolutely a game, filled with rules and regulations, effective plays and ineffective plays, mentor players, fouls, scoring, bogus calls, technicals, fast breaks, weak defense, heartbreak, defeat, victories, overtime, clutches, upsets, and more) sometimes we win, sometimes we lose, and sometimes we trade for a better fit.

When we win at love, it feels great! We give our all; we devote time and dedication; we show respect and are given respect; our allegiance is never in question and we keep the lines of communication operating smoothly with our teammate. We have a genuine bond with our teammate—there's mutual care, love, and support. As a result, the team has an admirable cohesiveness and walks away as champions at the end of the season with the prize—a healthy, happy, and growing relationship.

When we lose at love, it sucks! You give it all you have. You are so dedicated to your team. You fight so hard for your team—with your patience, your love, and your sacrifices—to secure the win. But time is of the essence, and there's the buzzer, indicating that the game (and season) is over, and you've just lost. Losing factors include: breakdowns in communication, poor timing, feeling underappreciated, lack of trust, poor foundation, conflicting goals. Your team will not be advancing. You're hurt, disappointed, angry, and even a little (no *a lot*) bitter, because in your opinion there was absolutely nothing more you could have possibly given or possibly done to change the outcome. You're frustrated because you feel that you went above and beyond to honor your commitment to the team. The only thing left to do now is wash your funky jersey, study the lessons of the failed season, and prepare yourself for a more fruitful season in the future. Preparing for a more fruitful season may include: establishing a more effective communication system, going to counseling, praying. Until your dedication and faith in the team dwindles to nothing, you're still willing to put in the work and effort required to win.

Sometimes in an effort to secure a championship, a trade needs to take place. It kind of sucks at first, but it always works out for the best. You were on a team with a quality player. You were a quality player. But for some odd reason, your team lacked the cohesiveness needed to make it very far. And as a result, you both had to go in different directions. You perform well with your new squad; plus, there aren't any ill feelings for your former teammate, who happens to be performing much better with his new squad as well. You both managed to turn the situation into a win.

Love has the same redeeming quality as basketball. There's always another game to play, another season to look forward to, another opportunity to try, try, and try again for more successful results. So don't become disheartened and hang your jerseys up just yet. Keep doing whatever is necessary—whether that be maintaining, rearranging, or team changing—to meet your dream of winning a happy, healthy, and growing relationship. #RedeemYourSeason

Love and Haircuts

s I sat in the salon's waiting area, *not so patiently* waiting and waiting and waiting and still waiting, to have my hair cut and styled one Friday afternoon, a thought ran across my mind: waiting for a great haircut has to be a lot like waiting for a great love.

I was extremely annoyed because I was hoping I could get in and out rather quickly. But just as with finding that great love rather quickly, rather easily, I was out of luck. I started thinking, *I should just leave and forget this waiting business*. But the thought of walking out of that salon and starting my much anticipated let's-get-it-in weekend—movies and drinks on the harbor for ladies' night, a cookout and surprise birthday party on Saturday, and brunch with the ladies at a new restaurant I was so looking forward to testing, or should I say tasting, on Sunday—with my hair cut and styled *just right* held me hostage in that salon. I exercised patience I thought had expired hours ago, hopeful that I was making the right decision. My thoughts told me to *just wait a little longer and a little longer and a little longer, because it will be worth it.* I became more and more frustrated by the second, but I suppressed those feelings.

As I sat there still waiting for the next available stylist, I couldn't stop thinking that this has to be *exactly* how waiting for love—the right love—must feel. Most of us won't find that great love without some patience, some understanding, some willingness to compromise, some feelings of frustration, and without wanting to throw in the towel but refusing to do so. What keeps us in the game of love anyway? Probably the same thing that kept me in that waiting chair much longer than I wanted to be kept—faith in a dream actually coming true.

PS: My hair turned out amazing by the way! It was *absolutely* worth the wait!

Not Falling in Love with the Put Down

On my way back from the gym, Brandy's song, "Put It Down," came over the radio waves. I turned the volume up and started swaying my head from side to side, totally unconcerned about possible onlookers. Then the chorus comes in: "If you put it down right, maybe we can fall in love." All of a sudden, the song kind of lost some of its appeal. If. You. Put. It. Down. Right. Maybe. We. Can. Fall. In. Love. Hmmm. Are we falling in love with the "put down" ladies? When we fall in love, we should be falling in love with substance; a man's honesty, his loyalty, his ethics and morals, his respect for us, his integrity,

how he loves the Lord, and his caring spirit. And
if he happens to one day "put it down right," then
that'll just be sweet and yummy icing on the cake.
#FallingInLoveWithSubstance

My First True Love

W hen I think of my first true love, so many adjectives come to mind: hilarious, loving, caring, chivalrous, charming, selfless, honest, reliable, generous, doting, and supportive. I never had to wonder or question what I meant to my first true love. He always made me feel so special, so loved, and so wanted with his sweet words of encouragement and affectionate gestures. I never had to chase my first love for quality time because he was never too busy for me. He'd make time to come to my games and coach me from the bleachers. And if my team got blown out and my performance was less than memorable, he'd always have a few words to lift my spirits back up, making me feel like a champ again. He'd prepare special dinners (split-pea soup and hot dogs—less than gourmet, but no less special) for me despite being exhausted from a hard day of work. I never had to wonder if my first true love really loved me, for he showed me daily with his actions—always making sure I had a few dollars in my pocket, not allowing anybody to mistreat or disrespect me, being my biggest cheerleader and my biggest fan.

My first true love was so giving, and the amazing part about it is that he never asked for anything in return. He was perfectly content with pouring his everything—love, patience, time, care—into me without reciprocity. And the sad thing about it is, even if I tried a million times over, I'd never be able to fully reciprocate all that he gave back to him. I feel so blessed to have experienced this type of love; other loves have stepped up to the plate and tried, at best, to match my first true love experience. However, they've all fallen short, and in some cases *extremely* short. Maybe they're right when they say you only get one true love.

My first true love had a way of making others seem like nonfactors. He made a little brown girl from the East Side of Buffalo, New York, feel like a princess amongst the royals of royalty. How can this kind of love ever be duplicated? My first true love wasn't just a man, he was a champion—my champion!

Happy Father's Day to my first true love—my dad!

Don't Just "Lay Down"...
Standard Up!

*L*adies, what has fooled us into thinking we can handle being just a Good-Enough-For-The-Sheets Chick? Trying to fool ourselves into thinking we don't want more than an occasional meeting of the bodies. Trying to fool ourselves into thinking being taken out on dates and treated like a lady isn't all that important. Trying to fool ourselves into thinking commitment isn't significant. We're sharing our time, our space, our bodies (our precious temples) with men who are more than willing to take us up on our sharing without commitment offers. Why? Who deemed commitment a naughty word? Why give him an easy pass to indulge in your deliciousness and take of your spirit when he isn't emphatic about respecting, caring for, and being with you...just you? Why give him the green light to indulge in your deliciousness while indulging in Honey Over Here and Honey Over There's deliciousness as well? Low standards and low expectations seem to be winning the battle. Where have our standards run off to? And when will they be returning?

When we stop the foolery and agree to be painfully honest with ourselves, something will eventually happen. True Feelings will stop by to pay a visit—a take-your-shoes-off, put-your-feet-up, would-you-like-something-to-eat-or-drink, you-can-sleep-in-the-guest-room type of visit. True Feelings shoots it straight. *She* speaks honestly and effectively, forcing us to listen. She speaks to us in a variety of ways: whispers, late-night tossing and turning, racing thoughts, stress headaches, sadness, weight loss, weight gain, and tears. True Feelings is trying to tell us that dishing out free dibs for temporary late-night thrills is some bull (in my Bernie Mac voice). She's trying to tell us that we're not setting high enough standards for how we're to be treated. Setting high standards and expectations translates as follows: Mr. Man, you will NOT joyride on my watch! Setting standards means the joyride is over, and that you're not *allowing* anyone to take you around and around in circles. And if he doesn't have the capacity to meet elevated standards, he probably shouldn't be meeting you between the sheets.

Ladies, anybody can "lay down," but knowing your worth forces you to "standard up." #GetYourStandardsUp

Teachers

I took a stroll down Relationship Memory Lane this morning. I took a moment to reflect on all the fellas who were simply not destined to go the distance with me. And although they didn't last, they all brought something meaningful, something valuable, to my life—lessons.

There's the college sweet/sourheart, who through his arrogance and controlling ways taught me to stand up for myself. Then there's the boo-turned-friend who, through his surprising and lousy display of love and care for me, taught me that I don't ever have to remain in a situation where I'm not treated in the absolute best regard; that I don't have to settle for being tolerated when I should be celebrated; that I can pack my bags and keep it pushing at any given moment. Then there's the momma's boy, who through his lack of ambition, taught me to always chase and work hard for what I want. Then there's the one who shall remain title-less, who taught me that the most important relationship I could ever invest in is my relationship with God. The demise of this relationship put me back on the map of my spiritual journey. This relationship taught me that God—not a man, not a situation, not possessions, nor titles—is my everything! Then there's the liar/BS artist who had a very short shelf life, and who taught me to always, always trust my gut, listen to the whispers, and that my intuition is one of my greatest gifts.

With all this said, I hold no grudges against my former "teachers." For although they may have caused this chica to release a few tears, I can't thank them enough for the lessons (blessings) they brought into my life. #GoodLookingOutGuys.

I Promise

*L*ovely ladies, it's so easy to feel beat down and discouraged after yet another disappointment, hurt, or knock-down. These disappointments, hurts, and knock-downs leave us feeling unworthy and of little value. It is in these moments when we must dig deep and encourage ourselves and when we must not surrender to the lies being told that we're no good or will never be good enough. We have to fight real hard to stomp untruths right out of our thoughts.

Promise, today and always, to never accept a lie about you as the truth. Promise, today and always, that despite the situation—a breakup, a cheating man, a checked-out mate—you'll always seek the beauty in yourself first, prior to allowing the situation to define and tell you who you are. Promise, today and always, to love yourself so much that thoughts of feeling unworthy won't even possess the power to penetrate your self-love armor.

Promise, today and always, to be your own #1 fan, your own biggest cheerleader, and your own motivational speaker. Promise, today and always, to actively look for and find the good and the amazing in yourself. Promise, today and always, to positively affirm yourself—I am valuable; I am significant; I am beautiful; I am lovable; I am worthy— each day. Promise, today and always, to embrace God's truth about you and to reject the foolish, inaccurate, and without-basis lies that for some unfathomable reason want to keep you bound. #IWillNotBeBoundByLies

Face Your Fears, Because You're Worth It!

Ladies, sometimes we dig our claws in and hold on so tightly, so frantically, to a guy who's not deserving of our love. And not so much because we love him dearly, but rather because we are terrified of what life will look like without him. We're too afraid to risk the SMALL portion of joy and peace we may occasionally experience with said person for birthright and ABUNDANT peace and joy. We give God a vote of no confidence in these situations. Not believing that God will provide us with everything we need (and for good measure He'll give us some of the things we want). We give ourselves a vote of no confidence in these situations also. Not believing in ourselves enough to trust that we're equipped to not only face our fears but to also conquer them. And because of this lack of confidence in ourselves, we hold on to foolishness, poor treatment, a lack of love, frustration, sad living, and confusion—making ourselves slaves to our fears.

A six year old said it best when she said, "Sometimes you have to face your fears, because everything is not as scary as you think." I say, you have to face your fears because you're worth it! You're worth everything that's waiting for you—peace, good times, joy, laughter, great health, happy living, love, and more—on the other side of your fears.

Dear Beautiful Woman,

I am truly grateful for and forever indebted to you for your purchase of and attention to Boy Bye! It is my sincerest hope that the words and messages in this book positively serve you, in some fashion, along your journey. May you always, despite circumstance, remember how special, unique, valuable, and beautiful you truly are.

Love always,

R. Hall

57987114R00138

Made in the USA
Charleston, SC
29 June 2016